The Fractured Zeitgeist

A Polemic on Post-Enlightenment

AF519337

Nadakkavu, Kozhikode, Kerala, 673011
www.insightpublica.com
e-mail: insightpublica@gmail.com
Title: **The Fractured Zeitgeist**
A Polemic on Post-Enlightement
Author: **Niranjan Krishnan**
First Edition: March 2024

Printed and Published by
InsightinPublica Printers & Publishers Pvt. Ltd.
ISBN 978-93-5517-609-7

The Fractured Zeitgeist

A Polemic on Post-Enlightenment

Niranjan Krishna

INSIGHT PUBLICA®

19-year-old. Currently working as a Robotics Engineer.
Parents: O. K. Murali Krishnan & Vidhya G Nair.
Brother: Darsan Krishna

Niranjan Krishna.

To Tiara,

For promises are to be kept.

Acknowledgements

To my Father, in helping me publish the work, finding the right reviewers and being meticulously thorough in the process.

To my Mother, who offered moral support, ironically to an amoralist son.

To Revathy Ayengar, for providing early feedback and understanding my philosophy.

To Arjun O.K, Eric Stucky, Abhinand Gireesh, Adhi Sankar, George Panicker-for your support, kindness to the alien and love.

To my therapist, Dr. Ashwini Viswanathan, for being maximally competent at your job such that it allowed me to look beyond my neurosis, enabling the eyes for truth.

To Abhay Santhakumar, you're my best friend, you're my brother, and for everything-I love you.

And finally, but by no means least, to my mentor, the Hermit of Sils Maria, Friedrich Wilhelm Nietzsche – in you, I found an untimely peer. Alas, I must overcome you too.

CONTENTS

Culture

Transition

New Grounds

Culture

Prologue: The Fallacy of Experts

Writing this book brings immense fear. Non-fiction books are usually written by "experts;" those with recognized credentials on the subject. My lack of the like prompts concern: Will anyone listen at all? Ultimately, all pursuits of greatness are those of acceptance in disguise.

As such, I should defend the question-Why read this at all? Why heed my words-who is ineligible to write philosophy from a normative third-person perspective-on the criticism of the dominant philosophical ideas that permeate and drive society? I claim that we have placed excessive importance on the idea of experts. And I must dismantle it to move forward. Therefore, I present to you-The Fallacy of Experts.

Philosophical Qualms on Appeal to Authority

In 1923, prominent American Zoologist Theophilus Painter declared, following his laboratory experiments, that humans have 24 pairs of chromosomes. Until 1956, this number was unquestioned among scientists, solely based on reverence for Painter's authority in the field. Even after subsequent experiments revealed the correct number (23), the confirmation bias remained. Scientists modified data to align with Painter's findings and biology textbooks with illustrations of 23 pairs of chromosomes declared the correct number to be 24.

From a purely philosophical perspective, appealing to experts is inherently fallacious. Consider the general form of the argument -

Person(s) A claim that X (the proposition) is true

Person(s) are experts

Thus, X (the proposition) is true

Authority is a product of social function. Particularly in subjects without solid foundations, like the humanities. In science, the case turns out to be different. Take Copernicus or even Mendel. The skepticism for their theories emerged from inferior experiments and as a result: a lack of replication of results. Indeed there was pushback from the Church, in the case of Copernicus, but once Galileo arrived at similar conclusions (through the Telescope) the scientific community accepted the ideas. This stemmed from a rough understanding of the scientific method back then. At least, as much required at the time.

More accurately, philosophy (and other social sciences) have no abstract methodological authority to fall back on. Its most pivotal problems still continue to be subjects of ongoing debate.

You're on a trolley moving 90 miles per hour. In front of you, two tracks stretch into the distance. The current track has five people tied to it-at the hands of whatever psychopath capable of such an act. The dusty sidetrack, however, has one individual fastened to the rails. Controls of the trolley amount to a lever and a note. Pull the lever to switch tracks, the note indicates.

As the trolley approaches the railroad switch, you hear voices from both sides of the track. Along the sidetrack stands a well-dressed Englishman. Switch tracks for the common good. After all, five is greater than one-Bentham shouts. However, a thick German accent persuades your ears to the other side. A rather short individual, with immaculate hairdo, in majestic dialect starts speaking. You shan't kill another, for that is your moral duty. Would you want another to change tracks, say if you were the one? Kant delivers.

It's maximally confusing and there's little time. The trolley accelerates to the point of no return. Suddenly, you wake up from the dream, sweat drenching your shirt.

Should I pull the lever-for the greater good? Or does my deontological duty forbid me from taking a life? Ironically, for Foot-who proposed the trolley problem (Foot 1967)-it was precisely this absurdity of Modern (post-enlightenment) morality she wanted to point out.

Foundations of, or lack thereof, Academia

In academic subjects without a solid foundation, the value of expertise is questionable. This is true for most social sciences and nearly all of modern academic philosophy. The social sciences are a battleground of competing theories with no consensus amongst them. Consider International Relations. Do we view states as key actors in an anarchic strategic battleground (Realism)? Or do we pursue peace and global cooperation as a universal humanist community (Liberalism)? Is it shaped by social norms (Constructivism) or self-interest-driven rational choices (Rational Choice)? Expert opinions are only as valid as the underlying assumptions. Reject the assumptions, and you reject the whole opinion.

As mentioned previously, philosophy suffers from a similar issue but on a larger scale. Furthermore, nobody seems to care enough to make an effort to solve these issues. It is well-known that past philosophers, including Hegel, Kant, and Aristotle, have attempted to solve these issues, but have been largely unsuccessful. Modern philosophers are reluctant to face failure. A project of such magnitude is bound to entail failure, and possibly only failure without any hope of success in sight.

The hard problem of consciousness is perhaps the biggest challenge in all integrated disciplines concerning the study of the human mind. What is consciousness? More explicitly, what is the relation between the physical states of the human brain and phenomenal experiences like color, emotions, and other qualia?

Behaviorism, the dominant school of thought in psychology, characterizes human behavior based on empirical stimuli and its processes. At a point where empiricism is insufficient to explain consciousness, founding psychological study on the former on an affirmative solution to the problem of consciousness requires a leap of faith. Not to mention the implicit assumptions behaviorism requires, particularly those pertaining to happiness, to function as theory and therapy (Cognitive Behavioral Therapy). More on that later.

Psychology, in its ideal form, would be an extension of ethics. To clarify, let's make the ethical-moral distinction, simply a matter of convenience. The Ethical refers to authentic individual desires and the Moral to the common good, if any exists. Psychology would then be the study of the human individual-their desires, their nature-paving the way for true ethical action. Acts of complete freedom, as far as it's possible.

The Peculiar Case of Faux-Experts

In the culture wars, as it's referred to, a central contention regards the subject of gender. While I adhere to a post-genderist denial of the idea, the nature of the discourse captivates me. Regardless of political alignment-progressives or centrists-conservatives-when an opinion comes up, people resort to asking the condescending question: Are you a medical expert? For centrists-conservatives, it is a way of resorting to the "biological sex and gender are synonymous" argument. For progressives, a way of claiming mental health improvement and progress for dysphoric individuals for whom a self-identified gender helps achieve that-according to experts.

Remark: See "On Gender" for more details

Interestingly enough, gender is not a biological concept or one in empirical science. In her seminal work The Second Sex (Beauvoir, 1949), Simone de Beauvoir introduces the sex-gender distinction. Essentially, while sex involves an individual's biological sexual traits, gender encompasses the behavioral and character traits that society expects based on these biological markers. The latter is exclusively a social subject, inapplicable to be studied through the lens of biology.

Faux-Expertise: When experts from one field are expected to have the correct answers to a seemingly related field that may, in fact, have no real connection

Another case arises when physicists are expected to provide correct answers to metaphysical questions. However science, by its nature, avoids the metaphysical realm. Physicalism is the metaphysical theory that asserts everything to be physical and thus knowable through empirical investigation. Science, or more accurately, the Scientific Method doesn't hinge on this axiom. Yet, physicalism is the accepted metaphysical worldview in the scientific community. There is no faulting them for their natural inclination towards it. However, exactly due to such acceptance, the general consensus of modern culture dictates the same.

Adding to the previous remarks on the appeal to authority, it's worth noting that Carl Sagan, perhaps the most prolific popularizer of Science, detested such arguments.

"One of the great commandments of science is, "Mistrust arguments from authority." ...Too many such arguments have proved too painfully wrong. Authorities must prove their contentions like everybody else." (Sagan 2011)

Ironically, it's now scientists themselves who often employ such arguments. Effectively replacing the authority of the Catholic Church with that of academia, albeit partially.

One must be careful of fighting monsters.

The Arrogance of Genius

True creativity can only be understood, its greatness appreciated, retroactively. And the greatest creativity? Never at all. For the idea is so outlandish that it is impossible for the current cultural psyche to conceive of its existence, let alone its acceptance.

Russell grappled with whether Wittgenstein was a genius or a madman. Nietzsche's philosophical significance only emerged posthumously. Even now, his ideas are not respected on their own merit but rather a reverence for philosophical authority. Van Gogh faced minimal commercial success during his life. Boltzmann's advancements in statistical mechanics gained recognition only after his suicide.

Am I comparing myself with those mentioned above? Yes and no. To some extent, I must. If I embark on critiquing, dismantling even, the prevailing cultural notions, denying any hints of genius-it would be an insult to human culture. On the other hand, I don't perceive it to be a special attribute. It's a happenstance, perhaps a fetal mutation, a random contingency. By some twist of fate, I possess insight. As Chekhov put it: If they (cultured people) have talent, they respect it. (Chekhov, 1920)

Many could label this as arrogance, and they might not be entirely wrong. Yet, there is more humility, nay, perhaps even maximal humility in my arrogance. What people often consider humility isn't humility at all. Consider the liberal perspective. Everyone has an opinion and we must respect it. When people speak of something, they start with the phrase – In my opinion. And the reason behind it is clear. Fear. For if you are wrong, or perceived as wrong, there is a way out – But that's just my opinion.

Ergo, the act of the greatest arrogance. One lacks the humility to make mistakes, the courage to face the pain, and the will to pursue true knowledge. Paradoxically, the greatest act of humility is maximal arrogance. If a rational individual is maximally arrogant, they would not discount the possibility of being wrong. Even ridiculed and humiliated as a result.

Yet, she holds on to the arguments. For after the battle, when she loses, it's humility that picks her back up. A step closer to truth.

The Prisoner Who Dreamt of Solving Philosophy

At the onset of World War I, Wittgenstein enlisted in the Austrian Army. In 1918, he was captured and confined to a prisoner camp. It was here that he conceived the initial notes for the

Tractatus Logico-Philosophicus. While the book was eventually dismissed, even by Wittgenstein, it harbored an ambitious and noble aim: To solve all of philosophy itself.

Wittgenstein held that philosophy, particularly metaphysics, stemmed from the misuse of language—where certain topics become linguistically meaningless to discuss. As he writes -

The book deals with the problems of philosophy and shows, as I believe, that the method of formulating these problems rests on the misunderstanding of the logic of our language. Its whole meaning could be summed up somewhat as follows: What can be said at all can be said clearly; and whereof one cannot speak thereof one must be silent

-Tractatus Logico-Philosophicus (Wittgenstein, 1921)

Though he didn't succeed, I share his belief that language is the key to solving philosophy. At least partially. My current endeavor, then, is undeniably ambitious. But what is life without a bit of grandiosity?

To conclude the note, I'm compelled to quote the two philosophers I consider myself the philosophical heir to: Wittgenstein and Nietzsche.

Here I am conscious that I have fallen far short of the possible. Simply because my powers are insufficient to cope with the task. May others come and do it better.

-End of the Preface, Tractatus Logico-Philosophicus

For that investigation one must await the advent of a new order of philosophers, such as will have other tastes and inclinations, the reverse of those hitherto prevalent–philosophers of the dangerous "Perhaps" in every sense of the term. And to speak in all seriousness, I see such new philosophers beginning to appear.

-Beyond Good and Evil (Nietzsche, 1886)

Thus, I have arrived.

References

Beauvoir, Simone de. *The Second Sex.* 1949.

Chekhov, Anton. "8 Qualities of Cultured People." *Letters of*

Anton Chekhov to his Family and Friends, 1920.

Foot, Philippa. "The Problem of Abortion and the Doctrine of the Double Effect." *Oxford Review,* no. 5, 1967.

Nietzsche, Friedrich. *Beyond Good and Evil.* 1886.

Sagan, Carl. The Demon-Haunted World: *Science as a Candle in the Dark.* Random House Publishing Group, 2011.

Wittgenstein, Ludwig. *Tractatus Logico-Philosophicus.* 1921.

On the Abuse of Happiness for Life

We hold these truths to be self-evident, that all men are created equal, that they are endowed by their Creator with certain unalienable Rights, that among these are Life, Liberty, and the pursuit of Happiness.

-United States Declaration of Independence, 1776

You have a serious ideological deviation at the very beginning of a famous proclamation of independence — you know, pursuit of happiness. If there is a point in psychoanalysis, it is that people do not really want or desire happiness.

-Slavoj Zizek on the Declaration of Independence

Happiness has been the overarching goal of humanity for some time. It's a hidden axiom at this point. The unknown known of our search for meaning. There is no why to the pursuit of happiness. It just is.

Ironically, those who chase happiness often find themselves less content (Mauss et al., 2011). This concept isn't exclusively modern; it has been a focal point since the inception of philosophy.

Philosophical Origins of Happiness

Although it is said that all of Western philosophy is a footnote to Plato (Whitehead, 1929), the pursuit of happiness can trace its origins back to Epicurus and Aristotle. Today, the Epicurean is synonymous with shades of hedonism. Although they are the same categorically, it would be inaccurate to label him a hedonist. At least in the modern sense of the term.

Rather than a frivolous pursuit of the highest pleasures, Epicurus is better characterized by a sense of neutrality, akin to Buddhism. Atraxia, translating to "freedom from worry" in Greek, was the materialistic counterpart to Nirvana in his philosophy.

In contrast, Aristotle's view on happiness is more subtle. As the creator of Virtue Ethics, his primary aim was the pursuit of the good life, a journey towards Eudaimonia. The exact definition of Eudaimonia still remains a subject of scholarly debate. Some translate it to mean happiness in a literal sense, while others adopt a broader, more vague meaning: human flourishing. If we are to be judicious of Aristotle, it seems unlikely that he would have used the word literally. Instead, Eudaimonia was associated with ethical excellence, the state of being that embodies the highest virtue, which he believed was necessary for achieving happiness. It merely played second fiddle to virtue, indispensable for its attainment.

Paradigms of Happiness

For convenience, I'll categorize ethical directives concerning happiness into two paradigms: the Active Paradigm and the Passive Paradigm.

The Active Paradigm is characterized by its primary focus on happiness. This perspective is reflected in the cultural outlook of You Only Live Once (YOLO), one that emphasizes short-term indulgence, often pertaining to drugs, sex, and food- the hedonistic version of the active paradigm. However, a concealed version exists too. One that distances itself from the former, on the surface, even taking pride in doing so, but ultimately reduces itself to the same essence. I refer to this paradigm as the long-term active paradigm, more commonly known as the phenomenon of delayed gratification.

Resonating more with Epicureanism than with hedonism, delayed gratification seeks to stave off pleasure and even indulge in pain-if it yields greater cumulative long-term pleasure. Recall my earlier statement about Epicures not being a hedonist in the conventional sense.

While all pleasure is good, he (Epicurus) says, it is not all to be chosen (and correspondingly for rejecting pain). We pass over pleasures if they bring an increase in further pains, and prefer present pains to present pleasures if this brings an increase in future pleasures.

Epicurus on Pleasure and Happiness, (Annas, 1987)

Consider the Freudian pleasure principle and reality principle. The pleasure principle directly abides by the Id (the unconscious instinctual facet of the psyche), succumbing to immediate impulses, in this context sexual desires and intoxicants. Conversely, the reality principle protects the Id from itself, negotiating with it and ultimately choosing what proves sustainable in the long run.

The passive paradigm follows the Aristotelian lineage of thought. As said before, the emphasis is on living the good life, the moral one, to attain happiness. Instead of directly pursuing happiness, the goal is to create the optimal conditions for happiness to occur and hope that it naturally arises. In recent history, one prominent figure who espoused this perspective is Frankl. Although he wasn't necessarily associated with either of these paradigms, as an existentialist psychologist, some of his writings can be analyzed to illustrate this point. In contrast to Aristotle, Frankl believed that happiness is a byproduct of finding meaning in life rather than achieving moral goodness. It can only be attained as an unintended consequence of working towards a goal that is greater than oneself. Happiness cannot be pursued: it must ensue (Frankl, 1946).

The Jouissance Paradigm

David Goggins is a retired Navy seal turned motivational speaker, popular for his grit and apparent resilience. He has several normatively accepted feats of tenacity, including ultra-marathons, a world record for pull-ups, and his military training. Central to his message is this perpetual emphasis on enduring suffering and pain, such that only deliberately causing pain, for its own sake, turns you into a warrior. While this outlook might appear superficially Nietzschean, that couldn't be further from the truth.

Now presents the perfect moment to introduce the third happiness paradigm: the Jouissance Paradigm. Jouissance, a concept from Lacanian Psychoanalysis, involves deriving pleasure, paradoxically, from breaking the implicit rules governing the enjoyment of pleasure. For instance, Bondage (or BDSM). At face value, Bondage is simply pain; however, it transgresses this pain to retain pleasure for the individual(s) engaging in it.

Az Zizek points out, renouncing pleasure can easily turn into taking pleasure in renunciation itself. This is where Goggins comes into play. Despite his resolute stance against indulging in comfortable pleasures, I claim that he finds subversive enjoyment in the visibly painful physical feats. For him, pleasure isn't derived from the content of the action; rather, his satisfaction stems from what these feats symbolize in a broader context. His ultra-endurance accomplishments, rigorous military training, and brash talk communicate something about him within the framework of society-albeit an abstract societal construct, the Lacanian "big Other". He emerges as a warrior, a fighter, the toughest man alive as they call him. It is within this realm that he procures his wellspring of pleasure.

The Manosphere, which shares an audience with Goggins, provides several instances of this phenomenon. At its heart lies the core assertion that feminism and the left are engaged in a war against masculinity, and the sole strategy to counter this involves men embracing suffering to ascend to a position of higher value. In practice, this translates to basic exercise routines and the practice of semen retention. Once more, surplus enjoyment reveals itself: an excessive pleasure from the identity of being a "high value" man.

To be clear, these are not strict categories. People don't exclusively adhere to a single paradigm; rather, the lives of modern individuals often permeate among the Active and Jouissance paradigms.

It's 8 o'clock. Time to rise and head to work, especially if you aim to arrive early. You input numbers day in and day out, drained and perhaps half-awake, but it's a necessary task. It's an investment for your future, enduring some discomfort now for security and enjoyment later. Work concludes at 6. Friends plan to visit a club later. You decide to join, as there's nothing on the agenda. Drinks flow, music blares, and your fourth or fifth drink brings a surge of sadness. Perhaps I should call them, despite their usual indifference. The phone rings and connects. After ten minutes, you grab your coat. Maybe this could be a regret tomorrow, but you call a cab to your ex's home.

The individual, following a consistent yet unfulfilling 9-to-5 routine (the long-term active paradigm), later hits the club for short-term pleasure (the hedonistic active paradigm), and finally reaches out to their ex-partner, despite the awareness of the potential mistake(the jouissance paradigm), serves as a clear depiction. Note that these are explicit outlines purely for exposition. In reality, we are unaware of our engagement with the paradigms. Such is the nature of ideology.

Philosophical Argument Against the Active Paradigm

Before engaging in a critique of the active paradigm, it's worth addressing the shortcomings of the passive paradigm. Within the passive paradigm, the focus on happiness becomes inconsequential. The occurrence of happiness as an incidental outcome is subject to chance, influenced by external or internal factors beyond our control.

Perhaps such emphasis serves as a practical tool for promoting ethical theories, for people remain invested in happiness even today. However, at the end of the day, a follower of this does not intentionally pursue happiness as a goal in and of itself. For if she does, it is passive no more.

Now, back to the active paradigm. For the sake of simplicity, let's define exactly what we're arguing against.

Happiness Hypothesis: The Ethical act is one that maximizes happiness, or broadly any positive emotion, and one that minimizes sadness and pain, or any negative emotions

Let's continue with a lemma:

Descriptor Lemma

Lemma: A descriptor for any set of objects of nature , holds significance only when not all objects within the set align to the prescribed description.

Proof. Consider a descriptor for all objects in a set . Then let be all objects in set with the descriptor . Now, assume all objects in have the descriptor (as means of a proof by contradiction). Here , implying to be a tautology. Hence, the descriptor has no meaning.

Now, I will argue that the value of happiness stems solely from its antithesis: the existence of suffering. Happiness is happiness precisely suffering exists. In the argument that follows, happiness corresponds to the good, while suffering corresponds with the bad.

Assume a world with no bad events. Consider the set of all events E in that world. Here goodness becomes a descriptor that applies to all events to varying degrees. However, according to the Descriptor Lemma, this descriptor has no meaning in such a world, as it reduces to mere actions. Therefore, for the concept of happiness to have any significance, there must be suffering present as well.

The analogy of the number line might help in understanding the concept. In the spirit of brevity, assume there exist only two types of events – Positive and Negative. Imagine them on a number line, facing opposite directions, marked by numbers with increasing intensity of the respective feeling.

Assuming the non-existence of negative events, the former number line reduces to a uni-directional ray, representing the positive events. Note that in this hypothetical world, the only emotions that exist are the "positive" ones on the number line. Positive events are merely events now, as the characteristic of positivity becomes irrelevant. Thus, there are no positive events anymore.

Such a contention arises due to the implicit nature of the happiness hypothesis. The simultaneous maximization and minimization of opposites, of happiness and suffering respectively.

One issue with the number line analogy is the question of a neutral point, or zero. Note that the number line is only an analogy to understand the actual argument. Furthermore, our subjective human nature makes it impossible not to assign value to something. Comparable to the impossibility of thinking about non-existence. An *ex nihilo* contention.

As there is no neutral point on the number line, emotions can only be measured in intensity with respect to their opposite. The intensity of positive emotions is measured by their distance from the most intense negative emotion previously experienced, and vice versa.

Barbie: the Yes Sayer?

The 2023 film "Barbie" was inherently political in its making. A satirical depiction of the patriarchy as the Barbieland, a fully-fledged matriarchal society featuring commanding Barbies and subordinate Kens. Towards the end, Ruth Handler, who created Barbie, helps her make a pivotal choice: to opt for life as a human or remain in Barbieland. Ruth instructs her to close her eyes and feel, leading to a montage of images featuring girls and women of various ages. The sequence instills in Barbie the extent of womanhood, and on a more fundamental level, human emotions.

The sequence encompassed not just joyful moments, but also sorrowful ones, and many more. Even Barbie confronts the painful imperfection of the earthly world. Now faced with a decision, she must choose between earthly reality and the eternally happy, utilitarian utopia of Barbieland. She chooses the real world, not inspite its imperfections, but because of them.

Comparable to the Experience Machine thought experiment -

"Suppose there were an experience machine that would give you any experience you desired. Superduper neuropsychologists could stimulate your brain so that you would think and feel you were writing a great novel, or making a friend, or reading an interesting book. All the time you would be floating in a tank, with electrodes attached to your brain. Should you plug into this machine for life, preprogramming your life experiences? [...] Of course, while in the tank you won't know that you're there; you'll think that it's all actually happening [...] Would you plug in?."

-Anarchy, State, and Utopia, (Nozick, 1973).

Most often, people opt against entering the experience machine. However, this observation is not presented as an argument. It's worth noting that my personal belief leans toward the possibility that people might actually choose differently, influenced by the status quo bias—where individuals irrationally favor the existing state of affairs. As I've already laid out the argument, these are additional elements of elucidation.

Returning to Barbie, one observes a subtle hint of our innate response. It's an affirmation of life in its entirety—the positive and the negative, the joyful and the excruciatingly painful. Not the Stoical, rather the Nietzchean Amor Fati.

I want to learn more and more to see as beautiful what is necessary in things; then I shall be one of those who make things beautiful. Amor fati: let that be my love henceforth! I do not want to wage war against what is ugly. I do not want to accuse; I do not even want to accuse those who accuse. Looking away shall be my only negation. And all in all and on the whole: some day I wish to be only a Yes-sayer.

-The Gay Science, (Nietzsche, 1882)

References

Annas, Julia. "Epicurus on Pleasure and Happiness." *The Society for Ancient Greek Philosophy Newsletter,* no. 146, 1987.

Frankl, Viktor. *Man's Search for Meaning.* 1946.

Mauss, Iris B., et al. "Can Seeking Happiness Make People Unhappy? Paradoxical Effects of Valuing Happiness." *Emotion,* vol. 11, no. 4, 2011, pp. 807-815.

Nietzsche, Friedrich. *The Gay Science.* 1882.

Nozick, Robert. *Anarchy, State, and Utopia.* 1974.

Whitehead, Alfred North. *Process and Reality.* 1929.

The Metaphysics of Intoxicants

Intoxicants intrigue me with their established subversion in usage. They are superficially condemned, yet are accepted behind the translucent veils. As Zizek illustrates, when parents advise college-bound children to avoid drugs, they don't strictly forbid it. Instead, the real message lies in enjoying alcohol, cigarettes, and even the occasional weed-although in moderation.

I'm not interested in the overdone and extensively discussed criticisms of intoxicants at large. Rather, my focus centers on exploring the metaphysic of intoxicants: their essence, significance, and impact on society as a whole. As we will observe, intoxicants are often completely encouraged. For that is the norm, the unquestionably accepted mode of functioning.

Physical Forms

We are all acquainted with them-alcohol, marijuana, and the like. But why do we consume them? Despite the well-known drawbacks to our faculties and the evident health risks and hazards, we seek a sense of exhilaration, embodied in the very word "intoxicants."

I claim that all physical intoxicants share a common set of purposes. Consider alcohol as a placeholder example. Typically, people consume alcohol for two reasons. Firstly, to cope with emotional distress. An existential crisis, financial hardship, or the most popular cause, as depicted by popular culture, heartbreak. Experience heartbreak? Let's drink our woes away. Secondly, it functions as an enhancer of general happiness. No problems exist, at least on the surface. A clear example of how the former reduces to escapism is when alcohol is used as a confidence booster. Picture yourself at a bar, spotting an attractive stranger seated alone. Anxiety sets in, accompanied by nervous shivers. A sip of vodka dulls your senses, impairs rational judgment, reducing the fear of consequences. Consequently, you gather the courage to approach them.

However, many instances of the second type are less straightforward. Say you're at a bar with friends. You've just landed a substantial promotion at work-higher pay, better office, and so on. Alcohol as a meansas means of celebration swiftly propels the joyous occasion into a euphoric one. Even this instance is a concealed form of shrewd escapism.

Consider the individual who currently resides at some level of happiness. They seek a peak, a maximal tip of elation. However, this pursuit comes at a cost, both to their body and mind. Isolated ethically, the action contradicts what they genuinely desire. Furthermore, referring back to the previous chapter, humans do not inherently desire happiness, therefore any form of exhilaration. Thus, we encounter an unethical action that entails a negative ethical consequence.

The existing level of happiness for the individual is insufficient, as they strive for a higher state of elation. This insufficiency directly reflects their discontentment. An escape from discontentment, for all intoxicants becomes its vehicles. Of course, the discontentment itself is not the real issue, but rather a surface-level symptom of underlying matters that demand attention, such as trauma, depression, or any other related concerns.

As Social Movements

We've traversed from the evident realm of physical intoxicants to subtler forms, those that manifest as social movements.

The first one, and the most influential of them all: Religion, or more abstractly, true worlds. The Theory of True Worlds, notably put forth by Nietzsche, stipulates a distinction between our present reality and the actual one, harboring beyond our perception. The present reality, or the Other World, inherently has a lower value. As exhibited by the pain, suffering, and distress humans endure daily. In contrast, the True World, the realm of utmost value, envisions the fulfillment of our wishes, often being a perpetually blissful utopia. As a result, the purpose of human existence is to act in a manner as to reach the True World.

In Christianity, the pivotal archetype for Nietzsche's contemplations, the Other World is the mundane earthly existence. Contrary to the True World forms the eternal paradise of Heaven. The goal of human existence is to abide by the Bible, the requisite pathway to access heaven. Other religions, to varying degrees, follow similar structure.

A more tangible example is the phenomenon of hustle culture and its numerous millionaire gurus, guiding individuals toward their aspirations of wealth. The premise is that through hard work, which ostensibly differentiates them from the majority, and unwavering self-belief, one can eventually have luxury cars, grand mansions, and private jets. Complete economic liberation enabling life on one's terms. However, it is precisely the structure of capitalism that produces inequality. As long as markets exist, winners and losers do too. The (false) solution offered by myriad courses and programs prompts individuals to toil within the system that sets them up for failure.

Emancipatory social movements, too, can adopt such forms. Despite my sympathy for communism, certain iterations of it have assumed comparable structure. The notion of a communist utopia, a society characterized by absolute wealth redistribution and the eradication of all forms of inequality. Within Marxian theory, all disparities are, however partially, rooted in Capital.

Feasibility aside, the exact nature of the goal doesn't matter. Assume a social movement with an ideal end goal. Socially, such emancipatory movements are agents of dismantling societal intoxicants-consider Feminism and its effect on the patriarchy. However, on an individual level, it often amalgamates to fulfill the roles of intoxicants. The affirmation of their identities as advocates of the movement. In classical Hegelian negation, that which they vowed to fight paradoxically finds a place within themselves.

The Metaphysical Intoxicant

Now, it is crucial to establish what constitutes a metaphysical intoxicant:

Metaphysical Intoxicant-*Any instrument, whether physical or abstract, that distorts our perception of reality, typically by impairing our mental and physical faculties, as a means to evade suffering.*

Certain intoxicants of the form permeate the global culture. In the previous chapter, I have already discussed one of the unknown metaphysical intoxicants-the pursuit of happiness. Another closely related one is that of romantic relationships. While romantic relationships themselves are not inherently negative and often carry profound significance, the way we conceive of relationships, both in the present and the past, has been unhealthy. The emphasis on looking forward from one milestone to the next-a diploma, a job, and finally a partner-is so pervasive that it is portrayed as a cure-all for our problems. This perspective transforms relationships into the "whatever makes you happy" object of desire is truly lamentable.

An intriguing characteristic of all the aforementioned intoxicants is their status as our inherent "default" state, the unknown knowns. We implicitly recognize that the ultimate objective, the meta-goal of our lives, is happiness. Even if individuals deviate from certain subgoals, such as romantic monogamy, the meta-goal remains intact. It is akin to breaking out of one box only to find oneself confined within a larger box. And amidst them all, the purest intoxicant, closely intertwined with happiness, is Hope.

Hope in reality is the worst of all evils because it prolongs the torments of man.

Human, All Too Human: A Book for Free Spirits, (Nietzsche, 1878)

Hope is the secular god. It acts as a sustaining force in our pursuit of happiness, even in the face of adversity, challenges, and suffering. When anything emerges that poses a threat to our happiness, we turn to hope as a means to intentionally blind ourselves from the current predicament. The Voice of Hope whispers to us, assuring us that the situation will improve. That future happiness, albeit hypothetical, sustains us in the present. Along with it the very problems that caused the situation too.

What if we weren't perpetually happy? In reality, none of us are. Yet, we persist in maintaining this façade, this pretense, simply because we are afraid to confront and embrace suffering. In the movie Lost in Translation (Coppola, 2003), a scene unfolds where the central characters, Bob and Charlotte, engage in karaoke with their Japanese companions. Toward the end, Bob performs the song "More than this" by Roxy Music.

The chorus concludes with the reiterated line-"You know there's nothing more than this." Gradually, Bob's face reflects a solemn melancholy as the truth of the moment dawns on him. A meaningless night of hedonistic indulgence is all that he can see. Nothing more, nothing beyond it. He shares a lingering gaze with Charlotte, who seemingly understands his sentiment, but visibly forces a smile. This embrace of their profoundly sad circumstances propels the narrative of the film. Even the climax, where they share a kiss and embrace, required said acceptance to foster something fruitful.

To just be, that's the great privilege of man.

References

Coppola, Sofia, director. *Lost in Translation.* 2003.

Nietzsche, Friedrich. *Human, All Too Human:* A Book for Free Spirits. 1878.

The Black and White Hypothesis

Flatland, the satirical novella by Edwin Abbott, features a two-dimensional world inhabited by geometric figures. The story is a commentary on Victorian society, specifically on women's roles and the class hierarchy of men in it. Although not seeing much success initially, it was rediscovered after General Theory of Relativity was published. The interaction between Square, the protagonist of Flatland, and Lineland, a one-dimensional world, was used as an expository tool to understand the fourth dimension, bringing Einstein's work into prominence.

On New Year's Eve, the Square dreams of venturing into Lineland, a world inhabited by men, comprised of lines, and women, the lustrous points of society. For the citizens of Flatland, the square appears as a sort of shape-shifting being of immense power. When the square aligns with the one-dimensional world, it appears as a line. When it is tangential to the world, it transforms into points. Hysteria ensues and the monarch of Lineland orders the assassination of the square. At least, that's the dream.

Ever since, Flatland has been used by authors to conceptualize higher dimensions. Surprisingly, higher dimensions are not all Flatland can help us comprehend.

The Political Spectrum

Contemporary politics are often perceived as a spectrum. Divided into two sides: the left (liberals and progressives) and the right (conservatives). Imagine this one-dimensional political spectrum as Lineland. For the citizens of Lineland, the other can only be grasped as the distant, antagonistic rival. Sooner or later, the Square appears. Visibly confused by such fierce opposition, one wonders – Do they not see the branch? What are they, but leaves of the same kin? The branch, the kin, of Deontological Ethics.

Broadly speaking, Deontological ethics employs rules to differentiate between right and wrong. An inherent flaw with this approach arises from conflicts amongst rules. Assuming a set of rules, conflicts between rules can only be resolved if one rule is shown to have a higher moral value than the other. However, no such competent meta-rule exists in the deontological realm. Hence, the political spectrum also suffers from the same problem. Both sides of the spectrum arise from different deontological families that prioritize conflicting sets of rules but have no meta-rule to resolve the conflict.

Take Abortion. On June 24, 2022, the US Supreme Court overturned Roe v. Wade, the landmark decision making access to abortion a constitutional right. Five decades of legal protection remained under the mercy of individual states. This sparked one of the most polarizing political debates in recent history.

To clear any ambiguity hereafter, here's my take on Abortion. Abortion is morally acceptable, at times even preferable. If safely done, even third-trimester abortions can be justified. Even the most progressive liberals will denounce the former stance, as it represents the most vulnerable case of the right's critiques, the one defending the right to life. The argument comes from a different moral framework, a non-deontological one, that rejects the inherent right to life. The keyword being ***inherent****. As it's irrelevant here, to be discussed later.*

Consider the routine argument. Conservatives argue that abortion is wrong as it violates the right to life, while liberals assert the right to bodily autonomy. Both rooted in deontology albeit with conflicting rules.

In a broader sense, the political spectrum can be seen as a conflict between positive and negative rights. The left is typically concerned with the former, ones that are necessary for people to secure well-being, such as a right to education, food, medical care, and shelter. The right, however, focuses on negative rights, which restrict the interference of others in individual action, or even inaction. Thus, the shortcoming of deontology. Although certain groups claim to have supposed solutions.

Shades of Grey

When discussing a polarizing topic like abortion, people often express what I call the Black and White Hypothesis.

The Black and White Hypothesis: The world is not all black and white. It exists in shades of grey

The idea is that we should avoid extreme positions and seek a reasonable compromise. Additionally, the middle ground is seen as the unbiased position, because it doesn't belong to either the black or white extreme, but rather, occupies a grey area. This appears to be nothing more than timid escapism. Essentially, they lack a solution to a complicated problem and worst of all, are unwilling to try. They take the path of least resistance, passively listening to a multitude of opinions, eventually adopting a faux-nuanced perception of neutrality.

Ergo, we have the centrist paradigm. They take pride in their position, believing it to be unbiased. Believing you're unbiased may be the biggest bias of all. In contemporary politics, we often picture an impartial line from which all political ideologies, and biases, diverge. For the centrists, the ideal is to return to the line. Instead, I claim the line is non-existent.

As an analogue, consider Nietzsche's argument against the concept of L'art pour l'art *(Art for Art's Sake, n.d.)*

A psychologist, on the other hand, asks: what does all art do? does it not praise? glorify? choose? prefer? With all this it strengthens or weakens certain valuations. Is this merely a “moreover”? an accident? something in which the artist’s instinct had no share? Or is it not the very presupposition of the artist’s ability? Does his basic instinct aim at art, or rather at the sense of art, at life? at a desirability of life? Art is the great stimulus to life: how could one understand it as purposeless, as aimless, as l’art pour l’art?

Friedrich Nietzsche, Twilight of the Idols

We don’t live in a politically neutral world. The world now, and has been, politically charged. The important issues relating to systemic injustices aside, we are born with color-tinted lenses of ideologies. Those that permeate beyond politics, and race but some characterization of humanness itself.

Thus, the centrist fails. Our concern shouldn’t be whether we are biased, but rather if we are holding the right bias. The time has come to stop cowering in shades of grey and decide what’s right: Black or White.

For truth is partial, accessible only when one takes sides, and is no less universal for this reason

Slavoj Zizek, First as Tragedy, then as Farce

References

Abbott, E. A. (1884). *Flatland: a romance of many dimensions.* New York :Dover Publications. 19531952

Art for art’s sake. (n.d.). Encyclopedia Britannica. https://www.britannica.com/topic/art-for-arts-sake

Einstein, A. (1915). On the General Theory of Relativity. *Sitzungsber. Preuss. Akad. Wiss. Berlin (Math. Phys.)*, 778-786.

Garnett, W. (1920). Euclid, Newton and Einstein. *Nature,* (104), 627-630.

https://doi.org/10.1038/104627a0

Kaku, M. (1995). *Hyperspace*. Oxford University Press.

Nietzsche, F. (2008). *Twilight of the Idols* (D. Large, Ed.; D. Large, Trans.). OUP Oxford.

Žižek, S. (2009). *First as Tragedy, then as Farce.*

On Gender

The documentary *What Is a Woman?*, features conservative political commentator Matt Walsh asking people the question-What is a woman? His target is the politically progressive, the social justice warriors as Walsh calls them, the advocates of gender ideology. He opposes the idea of gender being a spectrum, establishing it as a social construct? Dangerous. Individuals cannot identify according to their whims, denying their actual nature. As evident in the climax, where his wife defines a woman as "an adult human female, who needs help opening this"-handing a tight-lid jar to Walsh.

While the film is nothing but an utterly incompetent strawman, it does identify significant problems with the Left. Primarily, how it lacks understanding of its own positions, even though they are closer to reality. Nobody that Walsh argues against is able to come up with a coherent answer to his question. Although the footage could have been cherry-picked to align with his thoughts, an observation of culture at large suggests the commonness of said confusion. Thus, to clarify-What is, in fact, a woman?

Becoming a Woman

The Second Sex, initially published in 1949 as Le Deuxième Sexe, is perhaps the greatest philosophical work on sex, gender, and feminism. Written by Simone de Beauvoir, the French Existentialist philosopher, the book characteristically turns the existential motto, *existence precedes essence,* into a feminist one: One is not born, but rather becomes, a woman.

Beauvoir pioneered the sex-gender distinction, separating biological sex and the social construct of gender. Critically relevant as how the current political climate is fuelled by a lack of understanding of it. Sex is the biological marker that broadly classifies humans into male, female, and intersex. Gender, however, is the set of characteristics, behavior, and traits that society expects an individual of a certain sex to adhere to. For instance, men are expected to be strong, dominant, and assertive while women are to be submissive, caring, and nurturing. Here, Men and Women refer to Sex while the expectations constitute Gender.

In a Wittgensteinian fashion, the conservative argument that there exist only two genders lacks complete semantic clarity. Implicitly, it assumes gender to be a direct implication of the sex.

Sex =>Gender?

Primarily, two methods exist to advocate for this stance. The first involves studies from empirical psychology, while the other centers around an unfiltered biological approach.

Empirical Psychology

The Big Five personality model (Goldberg, 1990) stands as the best available taxonomy of personality traits. Developed under the lexical hypothesis that any culturally important personality characteristic will be represented in the language of the culture, it identifies five broad factors of personality.

1.Openness to experience

2.Conscientiousness

3.Extraversion

4.Agreeableness

5.Neuroticism

Based on this, multiple studies have looked at the gender-based difference in personality.

In Gender Differences in Personality across the Ten Aspects of the Big Five (Weisberg et al., 2011), researchers analyze gender differences in the broad big five categories and their subcategories. While they found small to moderate differences, the distributions of traits for men and women largely overlapped. Even agreeableness, the trait with the most pronounced difference, mostly coincided. All other traits showed even greater overlap. Consequently, the modest variation by itself doesn't indicate a causal link between sex and gender.

Another is Costa et al. (2001), which surprisingly concludes gender differences are more pronounced in Western egalitarian countries compared to traditional, conservative ones. A correlation hints at the possibility of gender being innate, although insufficient for causality. Apart from that, a plausible explanation, as the paper suggests, is found in attribution processes (Weiner & Graham, 1999). In individualistic egalitarian countries, a women's act of kindness might be perceived, by herself and others, as a voluntary choice reflecting on her personality. Conversely, the same action, in a collectivist traditional society is dismissed as compliance with the social norms. Personality differences exist everywhere but are attributed to different sources.

A Zizekian example comes to mind: the Authoritarian Father versus the Postmodern Father. Imagine a father asking his child to visit their grandmother. The authoritarian approach involves a direct order, although visibly unfree but preserving the child's inner freedom to channel frustration at the act. In contrast, the postmodern father suggests the child visit only if they genuinely desire. But reminds them how much grandmother loves them, how sad she would be if the visit didn't happen, and so on. Essentially manipulating the child into visiting nonetheless affirming their false sense of autonomy. Zizek argues the permissive approach imposes a greater unfreedom, as they must visit their grandmother and want to do so. Apparent freedom of choice can, paradoxically, lead to increased unfreedom.

Compare this to individualistic countries and traditional countries. Even now, societal norms continue to shape expectations around gender behavior. In individualistic countries, women are influenced by norms to want to conform. On the contrary, in traditional societies, akin to the authoritarian father, room exists to express discontent towards the visible injustice. It comes down a main tenet of psychoanalysis-We don't really what we think we want.

Furthermore, the failure of empirical psychology becomes evident here. It merely grazes over the current situation, the Is, to determine the nature of things, the Ought. However, an argument of this nature is fallacious, as the initial contention rests on questioning the Is, the present circumstances themselves. It ignores the external environment, societal conditioning, and hidden within them, the Lacanian big Other, influencing the formation of Gender. It simply escapes the question and asserts existing presuppositions; for it must be true, cause it is.

As Oscar Wilde notes -

A practical scheme is either one already in existence, or a scheme that could be carried out under the existing conditions; but it is exactly the existing conditions that one objects to, and any scheme that could accept these conditions is wrong and foolish.

-The Soul of Man Under Socialism, (Wilde, 1891)

On Biology

I aim to limit my exploration of biology to the necessary, as it's not the central subject of the book and I have nothing novel to offer. Thereby, here are the necessary to substantiate our argument.

When brain studies standardize variables, such as volume and weight, no definitive biological structures have been identified as causal links to behavioral traits-excluding those associated with sexual hormone production. For instance, the study by Sommer et al. (2008), a large meta-analysis, revealed no discernible sex difference in language lateralization. This phenomenon pertains to the engagement of one brain hemisphere in language functions to a greater extent than the other hemisphere.

A frequently drawn object centers around Connellan et al. (2000). In the study, 102 infants were presented with both a mobile toy and the face of the lead researcher. Researchers tracked the duration of the infants' attention on each object. The findings indicated that boys paid longer attention to the mobile, while girls paid longer attention to the face. The conclusion drawn was that male infants exhibited a stronger preference for the mechanical object, whereas female infants displayed a stronger preference for social objects i.e. the researcher's face.

However, the study faced criticism for its methodology. Instead of simultaneously presenting both the mobile and the face to gauge the infants' reactions, researchers chose to display them one at a time. As Cordelia Fine wrote -

It is, I imagine, rather hard to hold up a mobile, and look at a newborn, in exactly the same way 102 times

...

What if [the study's lead author] inadvertently moved the mobile more when she held it up for boys, or looked more directly, or with wider eyes, for the girls?

-Cordelia Fine, *Delusions of Gender*

Moreover, no similar study has been successfully replicated since.

Neo-pronouns-A (Self) Destructive Linguistic Solution?

If gender is merely a social construct, then why use pronouns altogether? Doesn't it simply adhere to the same essentialism that conservatives espouse, one that pervades our social reality? Yes. Here I radically reject the idea of contemporary progressives. Pronouns are categorizations with no truth, and no utility, to them. Therefore, they have no proper place in society.

Although to be prudent, pronouns could work as a descriptive paradigm toward the truth. In our conservative climate, denying gender is unthinkable. Instead, initiating an exchange of pronouns, he to she and vice versa, corrodes the idea. Later,

Neo-pronouns further the process. Do they mean anything? Absolutely not. But that is the point. A division of pronouns into groups, then into smaller xiers and xiems, and finally into individualized atoms where they hold no relevance. And with it gender too.

Postgenderism: The Truly Radical Position

Now, I will assert a provocative claim-Transgenderism is conservative. If the normal cisgender binary grounds gender essentialism in our bodies, transgenderism anchors it in the brain. More abstractly, an apriori non-(visibly) physical essence.

Notice how it causes incoherency in the progressive LGBT+ sphere. On one hand, gender is something each individual can subjectively define for themselves aposteriori, after being born. However, the other is gender essentialism which fluctuates between the gender binary, albeit negatively, with hopes of returning to their true nature.

Once the fact is accepted, namely that gender is not a spectrum, clarity begins to emerge. If anything, it resembles a two-dimensional plane. The perpendicular axes of socially delineated masculine and feminine and the individual who can position themselves anywhere on the plane. Moreover, the horizon isn't restricted to the plane alone; the possibility exists to transcend it, to the extra dimension. A wonderful place of ambiguity where gender is impertinent.

The Indian film Minnal Murali (2021), which translates to Lightning Murali, is the typical superhero origin story. Except for the atypical temperament of the protagonist and villain, compared to the normal superhuman characters. Jaison, or Minnal Murali, and Shibu, the antagonist, both acquire a set of superpowers after being struck by the same lightning-bestowing them with the usual array of superpowers, including superhuman strength, resilience, speed, and even telekinesis.

On the one hand, they embody said hypermasculine qualities, nonetheless, they are the most "feminine" characters in the film. Jaison is a sensitive heartbroken lover, shedding tears on multiple occasions throughout the story. A detail of significance, considering the heavily stigmatized nature of emotional vulnerability for men in India. Particularly for a character positioned as an action hero. Shibu isn't much different, an emotionally frail outcast who is labeled as crazy, his identity stemmed from how the villagers ostracized him and his mentally unstable mother. The same factor of alienation plays a role in preventing him from being with his love interest, Usha.

Both strong aggressive persons and sensitive vulnerable individuals.

In Lacanian terms, masculine and feminine are unrelated. Although it appears misogynistic, reeking of "Men are from Mars and Women are from Venus", it is one of the most radically feminist remarks ever. The traditional gender binary has men and women opposites, still related albeit negatively. The progressive gender ideology has it in a confused cesspool, merely concealing the same negative relation-although one that is bidirectional. Lacan rejects any relation, enabling one to embody the complete masculine and complete feminine in him-her.

Thus, I deny gender. And I claim that is the truly radical position; an embodiment of the mutually exclusives at once. A Lacanian unrelatedness to the idea itself.

References

Beauvoir, Simone de. *The Second Sex.* 1949.

Connellan, Jennifer, et al. "Sex differences in human neonatal social perception." *Infant Behavior and Development,* vol. 23, no. 1, 2000, pp. 113-118.

Costa, Paul T., et al. "Gender differences in personality traits across cultures: robust and surprising findings." *J Pers Soc Psychol,* 2001.

Fine, Cordelia. *Delusions of Gender: How Our Minds, Society, and Neurosexism Create Difference.* W. W. Norton, 2011.

Goldberg, Lewis R. "An alternative "description of personality": The Big-Five factor structure." *Journal of Personality and*

Social Psychology, vol. 59, no. 6, 1990, pp. 1216–1229.

Sommer, Iris E., et al. "Sex differences in handedness, asymmetry of the Planum Temporale and functional language lateralization." *Brain Research,* vol. 1206, 2008, pp. 76-88.

Weiner, Bernard, and Sandra Graham. "Attribution in personality psychology." *Handbook of personality: Theory and research*, 1999.

Weisberg, Yanna J., et al. *Gender Differences in Personality across the Ten Aspects of the Big Five.* Front Psychol., 2011.

Wilde, Oscar. *The Soul of Man Under Socialism.* 1891. Prologue: The Fallacy of Experts

Transition

The Ethical Imperative

God is dead. God remains dead. And we have killed him. How shall we comfort ourselves, the murderers of all murderers? What was holiest and mightiest of all that the world has yet owned has bled to death under our knives: who will wipe this blood off us? What water is there for us to clean ourselves? What festivals of atonement, what sacred games shall we have to invent? Is not the greatness of this deed too great for us? Must we ourselves not become gods simply to appear worthy of it?

-The Gay Science, (Nietzsche, 1882)

God is Dead. At first glance, it seems to be a radical atheistic rhetoric. But that couldn't be further from the truth. German Philosopher Friedrich Nietzsche wrote this in the backdrop of a post-enlightenment world, warning us of its consequences. The advent of reason and scientific evidence brought upon tremendous progress while destroying the foundation of existing religious beliefs. Even Christianity, which served as the backbone of Western Civilization, had no answer to this event. Slowly the realization dawned in – there was no good reason to believe in God. Thus we dealt the final blow.

While religion has its problems, the devil must get his dues. It answered the most important questions of human life – those of meaning and morality. Sooner or later every individual confronts the inevitable why – Why am I here? At a point in history where we've realized the scale of the Universe and our place in it, the question of meaning becomes terrifying. Our ancestors coped by imagining worlds of unlimited happiness, blissful by nature and superior to earthly life. But that is no longer true. What is the right action, one asks – the abyss stares back at them. For religious morality has no foundation to rest, and we have no alternative. We're lost individuals wandering around without reason, unaware of what life is.

The Trolley Problem

In 1967, Philippa Foot published the paper *The Problem of Abortion and the Doctrine of the Double Effect:* introducing the famous trolley problem.

There is a runaway trolley barreling down the railway tracks. Ahead, on the tracks, there are five people tied up and unable to move. The trolley is headed straight for them. You are standing some distance off in the train yard, next to a lever. If you pull this lever, the trolley will switch to a different set of tracks. However, you notice that there is one person on the side track. You have two (and only two) options:

1. Do nothing, in which case the trolley will kill the five people on the main track.
2. Pull the lever, diverting the trolley onto the side track where it will kill one person. Which is the more ethical option? Or, more simply: What is the right thing to do?

-The Trolley Problem

As elusively hinted in the Prologue, the problem has two (modern) solutions depending on the moral tradition one holds. The Deontologist, the protege of Kantian Ethics, argues you ought not to divert the trolley: it involves killing an individual, an immoral act against the right to life. For the Utilitarian, however, it is a pure numbers game. Five is greater than one, basic arithmetic even fourth-graders can grasp. By switching tracks, an individual is murdered, "sacrificed"-a better word, but saving the five, the greater good reclaimed.

Although Foote argues for a solution, a virtue ethical one, resembling deontology but ultimately aligning to the utilitarian outcome to switch tracks, I propose a more radical interpretation. The Trolley Problem, if anything, shows the paradoxical and insufficient nature of modern (post-enlightenment) morality. Perhaps even the question of morality, of how we frame it itself.

An almost-trivial counterexample: envision your child, one among the five individuals, on the main track. Any deontology, however strongly affined with theory, will switch tracks to kill the individual. Switch tracks, switch scenarios. If your child was the lone individual, lashed to the side track, no amount of super-egoic utilitarian guilt would convince you to save the five. The utmost free action? One that's a necessity; a nod to Zizek.

Qualms of Deontology-Utilitarianism- A Short Note

I have no interest in writing redundancy. The same issues raised with deontology-utilitarianism, a singular object, representatives of the post-enlightenment moral fabric, bore me. The obvious one in clear sight: what, if any, is the correct meta-ethical position and which does it seem to favor?

How can conflicts be resolved in Deontology in the absences of a competent meta-rule (The Black and White Hypothesis)? What about its innate context-lessness required to operate?

You're at home. Your friend arrives at your front door and tells you that he is being chased by someone who wants to kill him. You tell your friend to hide in a closet. Soon after, a man carrying an axe knocks on your door and demands to know where your friend is, so that he may kill him. What is the moral thing to do? To lie and save your friend? Or to tell the truth and watch your friend get murdered?

-Kant's Axe

For Kant, the answer is simple. The Truth, and the subsequent murder of your friend. An "unsophisticated" critique at face value, but an inescapable one. And one that allows moving on to more important concerns.

The Utilitarian. An objectivist in self-description, founded in empirical facts(?), those that emerge from ill-fit psychology-of the evolutionary kind. Ones that fit their preconceived ends. A maximization of "well-being" and minimization of suffering. Now if it were happiness, or any other non-vague description, the argument ends here. What is it, well-being, if not happiness?

A shrewd manipulation of language to blue their incompetence, to delude themselves. If happiness, or any pair of opposites in general, what about the innate impossibility of simultaneous maximization and minimization of opposites (On the Abuse of Happiness for Life)? Perhaps that in its unadulterated form, the only form even, it can justify Genocide? Juvenile criticism perhaps. But juveniles ought to be treated only like juveniles.

Some moved on, to find new justifications for its revival, a desperate attempt to hold on to something non-existent. Rule Utilitarianism, they call it. Rules are to be selected on the basis utility (the utilitarian meta-rule); i.e. rules that, in general, maximize "well-being" and minimize suffering. Consider that it merely reduces itself to its predecessor, returns back to the perverse father of Act Utilitarianism. As David Lyons writes -

Suppose an exception to a rule R produces the best possible consequences. Thus the new rule becomes – Do R except in circumstances of the sort C. However, anything that leads the act utilitarian to break a rule would lead the Kantian rule utilitarian to modify the rule. Thus, an adequate form of rule utilitarianism would be, at best, extensionally equivalent to act utilitarianism.

-The Forms and Limits of Utilitarianism,
David Lyons

Remark: The Ontological Failure of the Categorical Imperative

Any faithful Kantian would promptly object to the (above) critique, of meta-rules. That the categorical imperative suffices as one.

Act only according to that maxim whereby you can at the same time will that it should become a universal law.

-Groundwork of the Metaphysics of Morals, (Kant, 1785)

Yet, allow me a critique (of critique) founded in psychoanalytic theory. We lack enough knowledge about us, subsequently enough autonomy, to evaluate circumstances in which an action may become the universal law. For instance, a person who is neurotically afraid of getting criticized, under the categorical imperative, will refrain from criticizing others. But that is not the best course of action for them, or the other.

Battleground of the Superego: Modern Morality vs Subjectivism

For Freud, the Superego constitutes the judge. An abstract coagulation, a psychic one, of our parents, environment and society; and one of its large partitions-the moral one, the conscience. Its verdicts are the origin ground of (moral) guilt. Was so-and-so wrong on my part? The guilt creeps in. Even if morality is to be assumed, meta-ethically, an action driven by guilt remains inauthentic and immorally intentioned.

After God's Death, the bare truth of the world is that of nihilism. Moral nihilism, then, translates into moral subjectivism (in practice). We are the fundamental arbiters of rights and wrongs, our rights and wrongs. However, a clear pattern exists in reality. A moral pattern to such claims of faux-subjectivity.

Here, Modern Morality comes in. The primary layer is the institution of human rights. Right to life, right to property, right to X and so on. But such rights are still insufficient, even in their strict adherence, for the guilt to dissolve. For that one must make sure to do no harm. For instance, a critique-perhaps completely justified by freedom of speech-still mustn't cause suffering.

At this point, I am aware of the libertarian conservative, the American one, who dare partake my side. The greatest abusers of freedom of speech, a false claim of truth and rights mere instruments to that end. For you God is still alive, and that's ample reason to be dismissed.

Should I have said that? After all, her beliefs are her beliefs. Who am I to question them, to repudiate them? Especially something as sensitive as religion. Sure, I didn't do anything wrong technically, but it just doesn't feel right. Maybe I should have respected her decisions, her moral views. There is no god, right? Subjective to each individual, the moral views of one's own.

A battle of two, a relentless tug of war. On one hand, one feels the sense of right-wrong via guilt; to not cause harm, to respect opinions. However, the reality of moral subjectivism complicates things further. The subjectiveness itself amalgamates into another rule: Every opinion is to be respected, simply because.

The Ethical Contains the Moral

Anscombe's Modern Moral Philosophy (1958) stands out as one of the most intellectually honest works on morality within philosophy. While she critiques the deontological-utilitarian tradition, among others, at the same time, she acknowledges the critical incompetence of philosophy (at present) to even study morality.

The first is that it is not profitable for us at present to do moral philosophy; that should be laid aside at any rate until we have an adequate philosophy of psychology, in which we are conspicuously lacking

-Modern Moral Philosophy

We lack an understanding of psychology, the study of the human psyche under half-broken assumptions about the empirical nature of mind is insufficient. Even if we are judicious, assuming a pure physicalist interpretation of the mind, an inductive study thoroughly lacks rigor.

In this light, I aim to make the argument against the notion of morality as such, for its redundancy as an idea. As God is dead, religious metaphysical foundations have given way into demise. Any moral system, therefore, must be non-religious in its origins.

Non-religious morality has to presuppose (some) moral psychology. For the question of our concern is one of Ought. What one ought to do? As opposed to the Is. Interestingly, Is is self-sufficient linguistically. What is happening, being done? No further explanations required.

But the Ought? It begs a question. What one ought to do-relative to what? For morality the answer: What one ought to do, as a human?

An innate nature of humanness is assumed. If you are human, then you hold certain qualities. What are the Oughts on this basis? The nature of the Kantian Ought was reason, although incomplete in its constituency. Utilitarians held happiness near and suffering astray to be natural, a hedonistic nature of ought, a "pure" depiction of the Freudian pleasure principles; sometimes a strategic one.

Thus, Morality becomes a combination. The nature of humans, found through the study of moral psychology, to which Reason is applied. At this point, I must make certain demarcations. Simply an exercise in convenience, one of arbitrary sense.

Let Moral be defined as follows: What one ought to do, as a human? Now another term, the Ethical. Even though they are used synonymously, let the Ethical be defined as something else entirely. The Ethical being what one, an individual, wants to do. Not the group, not the collective humannes, rather the One.

I make a radical claim here. The Ethical contains the Moral. Suppose there exists a sufficient theory of morality. Consider a scenario which holds a correct answer to the question, no ambiguity, trolleys and tracks not in sight. Here, the correct answer to the Moral question is revealed through the application of reason to our moral nature.

Now, take the individual. Assume a (self) sufficient theory of the Ethical. One that leads them to reclaim authentic subjectivity. Akin to psychoanalysis, but a far better one. Our hypothetical individual is one who has then reclaimed the authentic subjective action. If so, the Moral action should align with the Ethical one. For a sufficient moral theory captures human nature well-enough to provide answers to the non-ambiguous hypothetical situation. At best, Morality becomes a redundant generalization of the Ethical.

Ergo, no there is no relevance for morality as such. If there's a theory of the Ethical, particularly how to reclaim authentic subjective action, morality isn't required; as it is naturally implied. That is not to reject any commonalities of human nature. I would assume a fair number of scenarios would have actions universally agreed upon to be authentic. Murder for its own sake, a trivial example. In this sense, morality becomes a subset of ethics.

Every moral theory fails to address the edge case, as then I must fulfill the duty of doing so in a non-moral theory. Say there exists a psychopath, who doesn't share the common human moral nature. I claim that any action by the psychopath is categorically indifferent in both ethical and moral cases.

In the Ethical one, they refrain from it out of fear; of the laws, of consequences. In the Moral case, the above could happen. More likely, they would refrain from the action, purely out of moral guilt-the superego strikes again.

References

Anscombe, G. E. M. "Modern Moral Philosophy." 1958.

Foot, Philippa. "The Problem of Abortion and the Doctrine of the Double Effect." . *Oxford Review*, no. No. 5, 1967.

Kant, Immanuel. *Groundwork of the Metaphysics of Morals.* 1785.

Lyons, David. *The Forms and Limits of Utilitarianism.* 1965.

Nietzsche, Friedrich. *The Gay Science.* 1882.

On Relative Immorality

Monitoring the Future, the long-term epidemiological study of American youth, garnered attention of late. A component survey examined the political affiliation of high-school students. As usual, attention calls for polarizing particulars.

A discrepancy amidst the male and female students, an inverse one. For anything archetypally American, politically and socially, the binary diagonals exist: Liberal and Conservative. The female students increasingly started identifying as liberals, while the male ones as conservative.

To be fair, the vast majority of students had no political affiliations at all-the choices being liberal and conservative. What truly intrigues me is the online uproar among liberals. The dialogue materialized into one of accusation, as if the male students worked out a conscious decision to lean conservative.

While I reject conservatism, and liberalism-if not for certain overlapping positions, the incriminatory tone and the intentions behind? Epistemically incorrect and ethically inauthentic. Representing the accused with options, between good and evil, the moral and immoral. If they choose the latter, the allegations are justified. All is well, except the role of a conscious choice.

Clearly, there's discernible social reason for the change-a lack of identity. After the enlightenment, aftermath the obituary of God and collapse of relgion-atleast intellectually-individuals have flung themselves into social movements, niches, anything that gives them that fa(lse)int hope of identity.

For Gender and the like, Feminism has been that source of identity for women-and rightfully so. The movement has its target confirmed, the destruction of the patriarchal masculine and feminine. The latter finds its identity, even if in the movement itself; however, the void emerged out of the Masculine? An identity for men? No form appears.

Is the answer recreating a new masculine form, a 'healthy masculinity' as charlatans seem to capitalize on? Absolutely not. The absence reveals itself as the symptom of the deeper problem, the bloodstains of the Divine on our hand; but I digress.

Apart from the lack, the treatment of men without compassion, especially in politically left communities offers no aid. Such despondent men turn around, offering their hand too quickly; reeks of desperation that beget vultures. Bald-headed sex traffickers, cigar smoking procurers in rented super-cars, ones who promise the true world of the past: a reinstatement of the Masculine.

Note that I accuse no one. The left isn't at fault for the rise of conservative men, nor are the men themselves at fault for their entrapment. Nobody is at 'fault', so to speak. Societal dynamics, throughout history, are shaped by the unconscious-collective and individual. Aftereffects of the caregivers and environment (individual) and the contingent historical, political, and other social circumstances present.

(Unconscious) Action and Non-Existence of 'Evil'

In later chapters, I plan to ground psychoanalytic theory with rigour. For now, let's move with an assumption. The foundational assumption of psychoanalysis and all that has spun from it: The existence of an unconscious and its dominant power over us.

The Moral is contained in the Ethical, courtesy of the previous chapter. A redundant abstraction of the Ethical if anything. Therefore, if one acts ethically, one acts morally. Consider the contrapositive-if one has acted immorally (not morally), one has acted unethically. Why does one act unethically, in unauthentic fashion? The unconscious neurosis dominates. Paraphrasing Freud, a lack of integration amongst the conscious and unconscious.

Consider that the case, the unconscious as the pilot of immoral actions. Then immoral (evil) acts don't necessitate any 'evilness' of the individual. For we assume the existence of evil requires an agency of evil, a choice made between that and the supposed good. How do we confront the individual who doesn't realize, in fact, is unable to realize this supposed good?

Conclusion: nobody is 'evil'. To acknowledge a potential for misinterpretation is an understatement. Am I claiming that an 'evil' act, say murder, should be done? Of course not. Rather the observation that it isn't 'evil', as we understand it now. The argument against murder, along with others, is that in most scenarios the action arises from inauthenticity, that it is an unethical act. Consequently, there are always explicit edge cases where the supposed act would be ethical. For instance, a parent killing her child's rapist-a high chance to be the authentic ethical.

Critic and the Criticized

Now, a critique. A critique of those who critique. Ethical failure of critics as they negate and become the criticized – the target of critique.

How does social critique, as the above, work? An allusion to the ought, the (yet) unnoticed prescriptive. The commentator observes the working of the society, he makes out the descriptive, the Is. Perhaps there exists no ought. Even worse, the wrong ought. Nevertheless, a different anchor is needed, a prescriptive to direct us.

Every analysis must contain a hint of emancipation. Especially those of moral and ethical nature. An acceptance that we are, in a sense, the same. However, the criticized is acting against what it is, what it wants to be. The analysis provides an alternative, the correct alternative.

It can never be otherwise. The anomalies of (human) nature, psychopaths and so on, exist outside our moral nature; separate from the essence needed for (emancipatory) critique. If the critic and the criticized are unalike, the criticism is pointless. Only a fool condemns a lion for being violent.

Such criticism stems from resentment – ressentiment, if you will. Consider Slave Morality. Rather than espousing moral nihilism, or worse, an egoist support of master morality, Nietzsche struck not the act, but through the act, at its intentions. The moral act, more often than not, is rooted in immoral intentions.

For the slave moralists, ressentiment is the drive. To differentiate themselves from the other. Indistinguishable from the critic. Even the right criticism, can't hide the one who pulls the strings beneath it all. Ressentiment.

One must be careful as to not commit vice, but also to not commit vice of not committing vice.

He who fights with monsters should look to it that he himself does not become a monster

-Beyond Good and Evil, Friedrich Nietzsche

Moral Sympathy vs Ethical Empathy

Rejection of 'evilness' isn't synonymous to an absence of antipathy. Our moral fabric is twisted such that emotional expression is chained by implicit conditions. When one is unintentionally wronged, one ought to forgive, which entails letting go (forcing out) of anger, contempt and any other 'negativity'. Only when there is justification of 'evil', thereby the 'evilness' of the other, can we transfer that justification onto our emotions.

Another sheep-cloth of the same wolf, Ressentiment. Now, in the form of moral sympathy. The greatest deception of Morality? Not moral prescriptive for actions, rather moral prescriptive of thoughts, of feelings. We are supposed to 'feel' for misfortune, even when there is no feeling. We are supposed to love everybody, an impossibility for love; possible for any dilute superficial form that takes upon its name, perhaps.

It dons the cap of empathy, but it's merely the pitiful cousin in disguise. Lead by a desire to be seen as Moral, in the eyes of the abstract Lacanian big Other, the harsh critic of the superego-the putative moral judges.

A radical departure. What if our eyes confronted the truth, that nobody is 'evil? The wronged and the wrong have no pretext for justification, no moral war cries to substantiate. However, do we need any? Isn't the fact that you are suffering, that you have been hurt, in pain, reason enough? For it to be valid, to be considered?

Does it become harder to reconcile the pain, the understanding that 'evil' is motivated by neurosis, that trauma manifested in the unconscious only knows of a certain expression? Immensely so. That is the cost of empathy, the Ethical kind.

Dangerous Philosophy

Superficial critiques are to be expected for such an exploration of morality and its broken nature. Arrows will be aimed at my 'moral corruptness'. Does the truth leave an uncomfortable mark on historical events? Perhaps. The dark unconscious of an abused child, neglected resentful cultural forces-always a recipe for catastrophe.

To refer to the introduction, the high school girls have no innate moral choice in taking up liberal positions as boys do with conservatism. One of many hypocritical condemnations, like the vilification of historical figures on the grounds of moral superiority-Gandhi, Oppenheimer and America alike. Condemnation has enough strength to stand alone, so why not let it?

Such truths aren't easily digestible. A (sesqui)century ago, another appeared to venture into the dangerous. Into the uncomfortable, painful, desolate truth. It;s time to finish, see it to completion, or if anything, perish pursuing what Nietzsche started. It is time to do dangerous philosophy.

People are too soon to judge an amoralist state of the world. Anarchy and Destruction will ensure, or so they speak. If we need the moral critic in our conscience, the practical consequences of reward and punishment, what good is good anyway? On the contrary, I am uncharacteristically optimistic here. The collapse of moral truths, the reverberations of the Death of God... perhaps the only hope for creative beginnings.

Are we perhaps still not too influenced by the most immediate consequences of this event-and these immediate consequences, the consequences for ourselves, are the opposite of what one might expect-not at all sad and gloomy, but much more like a new and barely describable type of light, happiness, relief, amusement, encouragement, dawn...

-The Gay Science, Friedrich Nietzsche

References

Monitoring the Future. University of Michigan, 2022.

Nietzsche, Friedrich. *Beyond Good and Evil.* 1886.

Nietzsche, Friedrich. *The Gay Science,.* 1882.

Nihilism, Language and the End of Metaphysics

As mentioned in the previous chapter, it wasn't simply morality that we destroyed along with God-but meaning as well. Until then, the meaning we sought through true worlds (Metaphysics of Intoxicants), eternal utopias and amalgamating into oneness alike, propelled us forward; more accurately, away from the painful truth. That our way of coping, one that practically emanated endless happiness, an invincible defence from suffering, had no grounds to remain at all.

From this emerged the philosophy of nothingness, of Nihilism. An extreme departure from essentialist sources of meaning to its complete destruction into the void, the abyss. Thus, the murder of our highest hopes brought forth other true worlds and non-essentialist sources of meaning.

The Concealed Nihilism of Absurdism

Absurdism, despite its digression from traditional philosophical methods, had tremendous impact on culture. Methodologically, and quoting Camus himself, Absurdism doesn't propone itself to be philosophy. Albeit its appearance throughout his literary works, *the Myth of Sisyphus* solidifies its non-fiction introduction.

In the book, Camus presents absurdism as a solution to the lack of existential meaning, to nihilism. For humans have an innate desire to seek meaning, but this is non-existent. If we are maximally judicious, it is something that cannot be known within human capabilities. Hence, the absurd arises-the breeding ground of Nihilism.

The Camusian "solution" is to affirm the absurd, as opposed to being disheartened in its presence. Affirming the absurd, or rebelling as he puts it, we defeat the abstract tyrant that has held us captive; perpetually until death. An apt analogue to the reinterpretation of Sisyphus -

> I leave Sisyphus at the foot of the mountain! One always finds one's burden again. But Sisyphus teaches the higher fidelity that negates the gods and raises rocks. He too concludes that all is well. This universe henceforth without a master seems to him neither sterile nor futile. Each atom of that stone, each mineral flake of that night-filled mountain, in itself forms a world. The struggle itself toward the heights is enough to fill a mans heart. One must imagine Sisyphus happy
>
> -The Myth of Sisyphus

Absurdism fails by adding nothing to the crisis of Nihilism. A linguistic critique, prompted by the Wittgensteinian in me. Nihilism grapples with the lack of meaning in a post-religious world. However, most nihilists go further: the impossibility of an "objective" meaning for life is taken to mean none at all.

Camus offers the prescription of acceptance, that the desire for meaning can never be quenched, thereby enforcing the nihilistic truth of the world. Here, return back to the question itself. Additionally, the question also posits the how of accepting nihilism, coming to terms with it and living life. The creator of sisyphus answers: Simply do it.

Absurdism added to the discourse of nihilism blurs our vision a little, but when the dust settles we face the same problem, in all its reflexivity.

Similar to modern cultural discourse, Camus misconstrues the ontology of reason. The prevailing narrative that "humans are rational beings while the univers, and life, are irrational entities" is enforced throughout. He accepts a less-intense version of the Jasperian notion-"[Reason] was driven by a despairing desire for metaphysical transcendence" (Karl Jaspers).

> Man stands face to face with the irrational. He feels within him his longing for happiness and for reason. The absurd is born of this confrontation between the human need and the unreasonable silence of the world.
>
> -The Myth of Sisyphus

Such supposed "irrationalities" transpires from a misunderstanding of meaning itself; that deems the major structure problem with Nihilism, more on that later.

Finally, Absurdism is the purest case of surplus enjoyment. An expository anecdote may help here. Once, a friend of mine got sick and bedridden. She was an avid fan of Camus and a self-described absurdist. At a point where the physical sickness translated into psychological despair, she channeled the absurdist notion of affirming the lack of meaning. Her dire suffering transformed into intense happiness, an almost mania. Taken aback, she felt and later spoke to me: if something has this much power to change my experience, could it be any different from religion?

Individuals who are depressed, existentially in the theoretical sense but concealed away are the psychological factors, change faces when confronted with Camus. A sense of pristine relatability and his brilliant prose sparks transformation. An optimistic individual, starkly contrasting their psychologically bed-ridden selves.

As it says nothing, the individual who applies the theory, nothing essentially, falls back to their existing neurotic patterns of behavior. However, this time a layer of unadulterated surplus enjoyment to shield them. Eventually, the layer to tears apart, its unsustainability revealed. But much like Sisyphus, they imagine themselves happy. And like the former, they push the rock up the mountain. A cycle repeats.

Linguistic Incoherence of Nihilism (and the Existentialist Spark)

Nihilism is a question of paramount importance. However, one has to recognize what "Nihilism" we are talking about. The actual problem of nihilism, and subsequently its question is- What is the state of Meaning after the death of God? More often than not, the question itself is skewed, resulting on a different turn of events.

The answers to such version take on various forms. More or less the argument that

The Universe doesn't have an [inherent|objective|transcendental] meaning.

Therefore, existence is meaningless.

Falling into the same pit traversed into by essentialist transcendental meaning. The only difference? Rejection of the transcendence itself.

When we speak of inherent meaning [relative to the universe], what does it mean? Can meaning exist inherently? Perhaps, but in relation to a subject that gives it meaning. Chair's meaning, thereby, is to be sat on; insofar as we decide to sit in it. It's not the traditional "inherence" that we speak of.

Hence, meaning can't be "objective"-for it always exists relative to the subjective being which allows it meaning. Consequently, the inter-subjective sphere beyond it. So far, this has been a critique of essentialist meaning. As for the Nihilist, rejecting the idea of meaning by the failure of an oxymoronic conception of it, both linguistically and philosophically, constitutes a misstep. Arriving at a conclusion, a negated one at that, under the guise of defeat-that of a non-existent concept.

Here, Existentialism touches upon an insight. As meaning exists only if a creator does, the subjective being in all synonymity, we can become the architects of our meaning.

Although a starting point, a spark as the title suggests, this characterization has further problems. Existence precede essence, on the backdrop of Tabula Rasa (Blank Slate) as the ontology of the self isn't completely accurate; nor usefully for such an ethical project, more on that later.

A hint exists, but a structure lacks. After the first step, the voices stop-we are lost, with nowhere to go. While ahead of Absurdism, in theory, practically the impact remains the same.

Everybody is Selfish, or Not?

Consider a seemingly unrelated theme, the usual adage-Human beings are inherently selfish. A common paradigm amongst the ideologues of the contemporary social psyche – capitalism, neo-liberalism, and moral subjectivism amongst others. Here I argue that this "enlightened" claim regarding human nature has no ground, for it misunderstands ideas involving meaning, language, and the self.

Consider the general, wide-ranging definition of selfishness

Selfishness: the property of acting, ultimately, for oneself.

Following the analytical tradition, namely of Frege and Wittgenstein, the former, a tautology, constitutes a meaningless proposition.

Similarly, the former reduces into a tautology. The subjective nature of the individual, axiomatically, requires them to act for themselves. Thus, this particular definition captures the set of all human individuals, precisely by the fundamental axiom implicit in its construction. The tautological nature of said proposition renders it meaningless. Hence, the question remains – What does it mean to be selfish?

Other claims on human nature, oftentimes, accompany selfishness. Particularly, one marking the optimal end of human life – the pursuit of happiness. When assertions about selfishness are raised, the former presupposition deems itself necessary. Hence, the definition of selfishness changes into – the property of acting, ultimately, for one's happiness (or pleasure). Then it becomes easy to reject the claim in question (On the Abuse of Happiness for Life)

Transactionality in relationships is oftentimes elicited as evidence of our selfish nature. However, this also falls into fallacious reasoning.

Transactionality of Relationships: Two, or more, agents engage in a relationship, setting certain conditions, ideally pertaining to their true nature – as to ensure complete freedom

The contention raised often involves identifying that relationships fail due to unmet needs or crossed boundaries. In transactionality, need and boundaries, ideally, represent those that align with individual nature. Using conditions that are assumed by the system, transactionality, as an argument for selfishness, while within it, is contradictory. Therefore, the fallacy reveals itself.

Explicating Unconditionality

What is unconditional love? The common idea is unwavering love no matter the circumstances. Oftentimes, the love is connected, directly or indirectly, to happiness. In reality, people refuse to comply with demands when it conflicts their boundaries. This is taken to mean a nihilistic truth about the world; that all relationships are transactional, that everybody is selfish.

Absolute unconditionality, as we mean it, can't be conceived in language. Unconditionality, like any word, can only exist under the constraints of its context. And the constraints of it? Boundaries.

Consider a mother and daughter. The mother loves her daughter in absolute unconditionality. Such that any demand of her child is complied with, under the justification of love. In this case, is the mother a free individual? Or merely an unfree extension of her daughter?

As Stefan Boros says

> Imagine your social skills become so good that you can charm or persuade anyone into doing anything you want. You become so good at applied psychology that you even have the superpower-like ability to control the tone of the people's voices and their exact choice of words and speed of talking. You can make anyone, with enough effort, do anything to

anyone else. In this hypothetical reality, once you become so powerful, how much of the other is "human" anymore? [...] Each person is a puppet of your decisions, and is thus controlled by you, it is as if no other person would exist, since you would only interact with yourself. To be unlimitedly persuasive is like playing a game of chess with yourself: you make both moves.

-Chapter XIII: Anxiety, Shyness and What Makes Us Human. In Love, politics, social norms and sex

Love happens amidst two individuals under authentic choice. If that authentcity isn't sustained, it ceases to be love. And boundaries are necessary for such authneticity. For if not, you cease to be yourself.

This is an argument for and against unconditionality. Against unconditionality, it wages that absolute unconditionality is non-existent. Similarly, it defends from the critics; similar to the Nihilists, they fight an imaginary enemy.

The End of (Absolutist) Metaphysics

Now, the latter – the End of Metaphysics. I claim, and plan to prove, that metaphysical claims are meaningless. An idea to similar to Carnap's, but rooted in maximal rigor. Specifically, metaphysical claims in the traditional sense-of pursuing Universals, Absolutes and the like. As opposed to the post-modern ones, Deluezeian theory for example.

Ontological Arguments

Although stated and re-stated again, different attires but the same content, the ontological argument has a rich "philosophical" tradition from Anselm's Classical Ontological Argument to Plantinga's Modal Ontological Argument.

Classical Ontological Argument

1. It is a conceptual truth (or, so to speak, true by definition) that God is a being than which none greater can be imagined (that is, the greatest possible being that can be imagined).

2. God exists as an idea in the mind.
3. A being that exists as an idea in the mind and in reality is, other things being equal, greater than a being that exists only as an idea in the mind.
4. Thus, if God exists only as an idea in the mind, then we can imagine something that is greater than God (that is, a greatest possible being that does exist).
5. But we cannot imagine something that is greater than God (for it is a contradiction to suppose that we can imagine a being greater than the greatest possible being that can be imagined.)
6. Therefore, God exists.

Variants since follow the base structure of the classical argument, the line of attack being the validity of conclusion on accepting the initial premise-There can possible exist a maximally great being i.e. God.

I don't plan to explain the argument, especially Plantiga's Modal Ontological Argument. Many before have criticized the abuse of the analytic-synthetic distinction, innate logical fallacies of assuming the existence of God, so to name a few. Rather, my aim is to demonstrated how metaphysicians, platonists of the like, linguistically delude themselves into believing nothing.

As stated, the argument basically suggests-If a maximally great being can possibly exist, then it exists. The premise is to be reasonably accepted, as Plantiga and other christian "philosophers" think so. A hasty assumption is made here, that language is a context-free universal entity. That maximal greatness meanis something outside of the context, none in this case.

Firstly, what does greatness mean? Clarity is gained when greatness [relative to x] is employed; the greatest [basketball player|musician|mathematician] for instance. Even they offer no conclusive solutions. But accepting specific qualitative evaluations of "greatness" to have universal solution-under, ironically, go-knows what epistemological foundations, what is the specific qualitative evaluation at play?

Is it the set of all qualitative evaluation? Is there a comprehensive set as such? What happens if elements in the set contradict each other, an inversely correlated evaluation of greatness(es)? Furthermore, maximally relative to what? As much as possible, but with respect to certain limits as it implicitly suggests. However, there are no limits here, a shrewd linguistic facade so far.

Now, the idea of possible worlds. Other critiques reveal the fallacy of equating possible world semantics as means of (modal) logical self-consistency to actual possible worlds existing in reality-that synthetic possible worlds exist. There exists one world where I drink coffee or tea today. But these are possibilities within one world. For synthetically, there exist one reality.

Necessary existence, another culprit. It exists only if the notion of 'possibler worlds' is to have any sensible meaning. Such that 'God' exists in all 'possible world'. Alas, Kant can do the critique much better than me-Existence is not a predicate (property).

The Non-Existence of 'God'

Like the former, all definitions of God have the same problem-a lack of linguistic sense. Take a common one: omnipotent (unlimited power), omniscience (knowing everything), morally perfect being. None of the descriptors are meaningful without context; sometimes never at all.

What is unlimited power? Is it physical power? If so, physical power-described by scientific notions, cannot be unlimited i.e infinite. It can approximate infinity, asymptotically approach it but not equal infinity. Application of contextual information breaks apart such 'definitions. Similar cases with omniscience, and moral perfection-a notion whose existence is unconfirmed meta-ethically.

Akin to the nihilistic response, the atheistic response towards omnipotence, if unironically, falls apart. Can God create an unstoppable force and immovable object? For if they clash, one will fail; either way 'disproving' God's omnipotence. Again, as context is applied to unstoppable-immovable they dissipate. If physical, the contention renders itself senseless.

To conclude, a note. This exhibits a small glimpse of how philosophical academia has failed increasingly. Discourse for the sake of discourse, opinions and arguments for their own sake, we have forsaken the actual pursuit of philosophy, that of knowledge. As Wittgenstein said -

Philosophy is a battle against the bewitchment of our intelligence by means of language

-Philosophical Investigations

References

Camus, Albert. *The Myth of Sisyphus.* 1942.

Lastrevio, tefan. *Love, Politics, Social Norms and Sex.* 2022.

Plantinga, Alvin. G*od, Freedom, and Evil.* 1974.

Wittgenstein, Ludwig. *Philosophical Investigations.* 1998.

New Grounds

A Note

We're here. The next few chapters are not comprehensive in terms of their topics of study. But they are new grounds. Swift, quick, cracking old rocks open and fostering the possibility of emergence, of new possibilities.

Much like headwater materializing into the gigantic river, it too will happen in time. Many still left to write.

A philosopher of *Gangasrotagati* knows.

The Epistemic Certainty of Language

Epistemological Nihilism – that which postulates truth doesn't exist, at the least out of grasp by mere humans. The Enlightenment and the collapse of religion, although a necessary step, has regressed in the hands of post-enlightenment culture. The question of God's whereabouts now lingers, devoid of an answer. The void stares at them. All hail the void then, so speak the enlightened ones.

The lack of epistemological foundation plays a role here. But where to start better than grounding truth in the very medium it can be expressed? Language.

Certainty of Belief

Take a belief *p*. The certainty of the belief can be, or has been, characterized in multiple ways.

(Absolute|Objective) Certainty

Historically associated with religion, but also availed by its replacements. Objective truth of 'God' and of God's word, for instance. The recent replacement is the 'objectivity' associated with science. Although, it is more a people problem than a science one. What new age atheists and scientism-advocates overlook is the necessity of metaphysics for 'objectivity'; that which (metaphysical) science can't provide.

(Absolute | Objective) certainty fails via ex *nihilo*. It has no 'sense', a linguistic critique once again. Absolute? In relation to what?

The answer-Nothing.

Uncertainty (Probable Certainty)

That *p* is true; perhaps. Epistemology, particularly contemporary, revolves around assessing the epistemic values of uncertainty(s). For instance, the epistemic value of probabilistic certainty.

For now, a binary categorization is presented-that between Absolute Certainty (non-existent) and Uncertainty (Probable Certainty).

(Necessary |Maximal) Certainty

The certainty that which is necessary, one we cannot function without. The certainty after which no certainty exists: the maximal one.

Certainty: Phenomenology and Language

What certainty is immediate to the Subject? Isn't it (apparent) that one feels pain here, somewhere in the body? Perhaps one feels sad behind the head, an almost-virtual abstract emotional space? An attempt to use language to communicate 'the thing' to other Subjects, the existence of which we didn't require language to be certain of. That is the realm of phenomenological certainty, the subjective kind.

As we venture to the non-subjective-the inter-subjective, empirical reality and even the 'objective'-uncertain grounds are found. I must follow the great skeptical tradition and start from nothing. A blank slate; a void.

What can we not live without? What faculty, entity or 'thing', is necessary that even the ultimate skeptical claim submits to it? Language. The skeptical claim resides inside language, in a language-game. To claim skepticism against language is suicide, a knife through one's body, a seppuku. Thereby, the only thing we can be (maximally | necessarily) certain of is language itself.

Assumed Certainty of Language

Consider a conversation between two agents using Language L. Assume a sign S and a signified O being used. When both agents use the sign S, they assume the other to be referring to the signified O. This is the Assumed Certainty (A.C) of Truth in Language.

There are degrees to it inside language too. For instance, consider dialects. Oftentimes, in a dialect d of language L, the assumed certainty of truth will be of greater degree than that of L.

$$A.C(d) > A.C(L)$$

More generally, any sub-culture of language has this property. Consider families where there are hidden jokes and references amongst the others. The signified becomes vastly different between the public and the private here.

Then, the Maximum Assumed Certainty in Language happens in a 2-agent relationship of the highest possible connection. Although, it could potentially not reveal itself in practical life, the highest possible certainty of the kind takes this form.

In any sense, studying the limits of epistemology starts with studying the limits of language. It involves a project that rigorously characterizes language, extends the search to its limits, revealing what is epistemologically possible; that what is epistemological?

Necessary Certainty of Language Theorem

To aid a rigorous formulation of the argument before, I state the following claim

Claim: Assumed Certainty of Language is equivalent to the (Necessary | Maximal) Certainty

Proof. Assume there exists a method, a proposition, or an entity or 'thing' that exhibits far more (necessary|maximal) certainty than language in the non-subjective sphere.

Call it not-language. To claim the certainty of not-language, one must articulate it, thereby evoking language itself. If one can't articulate it to other subjects, it reduces to the realm of phenomenological certainty-independent of the non-subjective realm by definition.

Thus, one necessitates the (necessary|maximal) certainty of not-language to be bound by the (necessary|maximal) certainty of language.

Hence proved by contradiction.

Conclusion

This is a prolegomena, a search that needs further study. A new epistemological project through language. Even as the essay doesn't walk far, that is the purpose of newer projects-to overcome the previous ones. And I not-hope to see them through to completion.

Perhaps the Wittgenstein dictum helps drive the point home -

The limits of my language mean the limits of my world

-Ludwig Wittgenstein

References

Wittgenstein, Ludwig. *Tractatus Logico-Philosophicus.* 1921.

Ontology of Meaning

In complete candor, this essay comprises theory. In the traditional sense, that is speculative theory. Assumptions yet unverified, but plausible-indirectly through correlated facts or intuitively, for the creator. Here is one of the former and the latter.

As noted, the Death of God demolished religious foundations. Consequently, (religious) morality and meaning; the human necessities due to the devil. An outline of morality, its problem and the hint at a solution of possibility has been given (The Ethical Imperative). Realization dawns that the solution to (lack of) meaning isn't disconnected from the former, that it forms the foundation of the Ethical. That is, the Ontological.

The Confused Structure of Tabula Rasa

Famously used in An Essay Concerning Human Understanding, Tabula Rasa (Latin) translates to "clean slate". For Locke, it served the outset of empiricism; the white paper forming the human mind, learning and generating heuristics as responses to external stimuli. The French Existentialists adopted the view, even extending it beyond Locke.

Existence precedes essence, Sartre's commandment. One that commands us to create our commandments. Man is free to create himself, give herself identity, unconfined by the presupposed societal archetypes. Sartre's focus, also this essay, is the ontology of the individual, not the normative state of it. In reality, the development of the individual is controlled by external factors. One is not born, rather becomes a woman-as Beauvoir points out (one facet) in the Second Sex.

Despite its literal meaning, the proponents of Tabula Rasa don't claim no essence-as that would be an impossibility. Rather the essence of white paper itself, a limited essence, the smallest set of characteristics that make up the Human. Something comprehensively addressed by Aristotelian Virtue Ethics.

For Aristotle, virtues are reactions to the current state of affairs-both externally (the circumstances) and internally (emotions). Correct virtue lies amid two vices, those of excess and deficiency. An adequate response, the virtuous one, to an external circumstance effectuating Fear would be Courage; that which is situated between Cowardice and Recklessness.

However, Aristotle fails in his extensive project on its own "merit". While the virtues themselves are not explicitly specific, the underlying context is relative to his time. In that respect, a lot of virtues are defined by external societal validators. Modesty, Righteousness and Wisdom-a few[1]. Like other conceptions of Human-ness, it enforces a restrictive view on what should be; rather than what we can be, a creative possibility to behold.

On Concrete Ontology

Modernity hasn't moved further from Aristotle. As with the Nicomachean Ethics, where the human essence was concrete, a set of exact virtues constituting one, we have advanced towards more specificity. The contemporary idea of passion, that individuals are born to do X (the passion) which remains to be found. However, that something only exists as part of the present-day cultural frame-Capitalism, for us. Those "born" to be an Entrepreneur, in fact if born as an African American in pre-abolitionist America? No such possibility could have crossed their heads.

As discussed previously (On Gender), Gender Identity rep-

1 [For a detailed treatment of virtue-The Non-Buddha: A Metaphysical Conception of the Virtuous Krishna (2023)
Source: niranjankrishna.in].

resents another limiting essence. Transgenderist essentialism simply returns to the flawed cis-gender binaries and constraints. Although to condemn the transgender movement wouldn't be fair at all, as Cisgender essentialism has been the accepted norm. Men and women have different preferences by nature, they say-failing to recognize the preferences themselves the product of culture. A trivial example? An affinity for race cars and guns.

Concrete Ontology, the formulation of individual ontology as concrete specifics, the products of contingent circumstances. One where the particulars of culture, time and environment are assumed to be the ontological essence.

Nature of Imperishable Meaning

If there exists imperishable meaning, what would it look like? Strains of meaning at our disposal are concrete but also predicated on outcomes. The most glaring example is religion, that of true worlds. Mankind has a singular goal, to abide by the commandments in hopes of reaching heaven.

Now, God is dead. But his shadows have produced other (the same) forms of meaning. Pursuit of a romantic partner (the Romantic Ideal), Accumulation of Monetary Wealth (the Capitalist Ideal), to name a few. However, a general structural problem emerges. Upon reaching the goal, the outcome, the "concrete" meaning dissipates. For the goal is non-existent, a void connecting meaning to anything (nothing) concrete.

In fact, the only warrant of imperishability is meaning derived from the pursuit itself. Thus, the nature of imperishable, the extent of it for humans, meaning-one of pursuit, one of becoming.

But becoming what? What is Becoming?

Flux Ontology

Opposites of the discourse of ontology-the confused emptiness of Tabula Rasa and the concrete specifics of Virtue Ethics and related quasis. What does the Zombie do here? The undead? The Atopical? They go beyond the discourse. Revealing the essence of flux, of becoming.

Individuals are defined by a set of qualities, virtues even, of becoming. The Moral Set, one that's common to us, one that defines our human-ness. Inevitably, our environments develop the set into specifics, oftentimes neurotic specifics. One also can't overlook certain individuals who are, perhaps the influence of a mutated gene or two, far more capable in certain qualities. For instance, the great creators of humanity-Picasso, Nietzsche, Euler, among others. Even slight variants are to be seen amongst individuals, certain families and the like.

The set outside, and containing, the Moral Set-The Ethical Set. Note that this doesn't avow away concrete essence. Rather a recognition that concrete essences are contingent factors built upon the essential flux; and thus can be molded. In the language of modern dialect, the concrete essences compose Goals and the essential flux Meta-Goals. To be a painter is the goal (concrete essence) of the mta-goal (essential flux) of creation. Creative painters, that is.

A Beyond-interpretation of the Übermensch

In Thus Spoke Zarathustra, Nietzche appears to give away the solution to meaning. Albeit not in a clear fashion.

The Übermensch shall be the meaning of the earth! I entreat you my brethren, remain true to the earth, and do not believe those who speak to you of supra-terrestrial hopes! ... Behold, I teach you the Übermensch: he is this lightning, he is this madness! ... Behold, I am a prophet of the lightning and a heavy drop from the cloud: but this lightning is called Übermensch.

-Thus Spoke Zarathustra

Even a careful reading of his complete bibliography remains insufficient for a clear picture. Scholars have debated throughout on what the Übermensch means. Is it something achievable or merely an impossibility? A superior transhumanistic being or one of increased mental fervor and spirit? The next step of human evolution? As Nietzsche couldn't complete his positive project, in contrast to the negative enlightenment one, I claim for a beyond-interpretation.

Übermensch: The abstract beyond-individual (relative to the real current one) who transcends one or more essential fluxes, in contrast to the present one. An ever-moving imperishable anchor that enables becoming, one that perpetually exists, as long as one is alive. A Beautiful being with limitless potential, invigorating one with excitement, affirming life itself

But, the project has only started. Questions remain, how to ensure that we are capable of constructing (our) Übermensch. In a culture of psychoanalytical unfreedom-neurosis and T-t traumas-Schizoanalytical unfreedom-the faux capitalist incentive ingrained within us.

That becomes our Ethical project. How to set the ontological free? Our next great pursuit.

References

Aristotle. *Nicomachean Ethics*.

Beauvoir, Simone de. *The Second Sex*. 1949.

Locke, John. *An Essay Concerning Human Understanding*. 1689.

Maté, Gabor. *The Myth of Normal: Trauma, Illness, and Healing in a Toxic Culture*. 2022.

Nietzsche, Friedrich. *Thus Spoke Zarathustra*. 1883.

Sartre, Jean-Paul. *Existentialism Is a Humanism*. 1946.

The Topology of Analysis

The Ontological Project is followed by the Ethical one. How to engender the Ontological, enable the individual to become what they are? Usually, the Ethical-Moral projects rely on prescriptives-often explicit ones-that direct the conscious persona to act. In contrast, our Ethical, resting on Flux Ontology, offers no prescriptives. Rather it allows the Ontological to emerge unclouded, to make itself prescriptives, foster new grounds for Becoming.

As the diligent farmer plows, fertilizes and sows seeds, anticipating the yield, what process is required for ontological emergence? What caused the infertility of the farmland, if anything? What are the forces that prevent ontological emergence, if anything? The Unconscious and Culture-independent at times, bidirectionally correlated, and sometimes a confederate force.

The Psychoanalytic Neurotic Unconscious, an existence acknowledged in the minority, but rejected in prevalence. As Maté argues, it is not merely Capital T trauma-post-traumatic stress disorder, emotional abuse and violence-but the small-t trauma capable of influence; the conditions not just wrong action, but inaction. Although the specifics of Freudian-Lacanian ideas are to be disputed, the fundamental holds true: that through parenting, we are effecting neurosis in children.

At large, culturally, the Death of God. Considerable factors of individual neurosis are not isolated to parenting, but to the broader cultural forces, both material and ideological. The Pursuit of Happiness (On the Abuse of Happiness for Life), the most deplorable culprit. When a child cries, the immediate course of action is distraction, an advice to let go, the reproduction of broken coping mechanisms. Somehow, conditioning the child to harbor an undesirable view of "negative" emotions and their expression.

Subsequently, the True Worlds-an existence predicated on Happiness and its companion, Hope. Collapse of religion, the original true world, offered a chance. To overcome human, is it not that what is Human? However, a cyclic fabrication of true worlds in God's shadow has perpetuated since. Capitalist, Communist Movements (20th Century) and the Romantic Ideal, to name a few. Even instrumental movements not inherently true world-esque, Feminism and Unionization, are performatively taken as one, attenuating its intent and authenticity.

In Deleuzian-Guattarian terms, the Schizoanalytically Unconscious. Assume one becomes aware of it, unlike the psychoanalytically unconscious, escape is impossible. Modern psychology, and its dominant strains-Behaviorism, Humanism and the like-are unequipped to tackle both problems. An incessant cry for scientific modeling, a realm where 'science', as we know now, is inept epistemologically.

Any creation must sow the seeds and light the thunder of destruction. Thus, where we start.

A Critique of Anti-Unconscious Psychology

Since critiquing all anti-unconscious psychological traditions is superfluous, instead the critique will center the structural assumptions that base them. Principally focusing on Cognitive-Behavioral and Humanistic traditions, and their variants.

First, the assumption represented by the Cognitive-Behavioral, the idea of a correct emotion and subsequent behavior. Any psychological dysfunction proceeds as follows -

Automatic Thought=> Undesirable Emotion=> Undesirable Action

As Judith Beck writes

> For example, if you were quite depressed and bounced some checks, you might have an automatic thought, an idea that just seemed to pop up in your mind: "I can't do anything right." This thought might then lead to a particular reaction: you might feel sad (emotion) and retreat to bed (behavior)
>
> -Cognitive Behavior Therapy, Second Edition: Basics and Beyond

One conjectures that sadness, or any behavior of the "negative" category, is inherently bad. As opposed to a lack of evidence for the assumption, and the clear incoherency of it (On the Abuse of Happiness for Life).

Now, undesirable behavior. Along with the fallacious conception of emotions, the undesirability of behavior appears to have a culture bias to the norm. Consider the cited example, the hypothetical individual having her checks bounced. It assumes the fairness of the system (capitalism), such that not showing up to work as the "incorrect" anomaly. A single black mother, three children and a convicted husband, living in a red state? Not much options present.

Next, the representation assumption of Humanism: Freedom. Humans are capable of intentional free choice, thus responsible for our lives. What does "free" mean? Not the abstract essence of freedom, a randomness, a pure chaos if you will. Rather free, the sense predicated on human intentionality, free to do what one wants. Desires separate from social determinism, the realm of personal ones.

Psychoanalysis shines light (dark?) here-We don't want what we think we desire. Consider an abusive wife. As she screams for help getting thrashed by her husband, upon the arrival of cops, she sides with him; that he actually loves her, cares for her and so on. A common occurrence in developing countries. A more American example is emotional and verbal abuse. The inherent de-contextualization of the former impedes fast legal action, making it easier for people to stay in the abusive relationship, maintaining that they actually "want" the abusive partner.

Statistical data from attachment studies confirms the same. If most individuals engage in relationships, ones that activate toxic parental relational patterns, one of our culture's most accepted aims of finding a romantic partner arises from inauthenticity. Finally, the normative philosophical argument. If the pursuit of happiness is incoherent (On the Abuse of Happiness for Life), no arguments are required. For if the anchoring goal of our culture, implicitly desired by most, is an aeration pursuit, the psychoanalytic assumptions claims victory.

In all honesty, I dislike such a critique. Humankind faces problems of extraordinary magnitude, that we are oblivious even in approach. An easier solution is making unwarranted assumptions and extracting conclusions-the story of philosophical institutions (academia). I say that in face of impossible problems, that the probable outcome is failure, one ought to fight it in candour. And if defeated, face our own incompetence.

Honest defeat over delusional victory.

An Epistemic Defence of Psychoanalysis

Freud has a strange posthumous reputation, the strangest of any great thinker. He established Psychoanalysis, and the psychoanalytic method, an essential aspect of non-psychoanalytic psychotherapies. Perhaps he was wrong about particulars, but that is not sufficient reason to reject his work and legacy.

In 1905, Einstein published the paper on Special Relativity, dismantling the Newtonian paradigm of Classical Mechanics. Such that, unlike Freud's talking cure, Newtonian Mechanics was no more a necessity, a practicality instead. Yet, there is no condemnation of Newton, and rightfully so. Thus, staring us in the eye is the Hypocritical, arising anytime we confront harsh truths. Juvenile critiques of Freud take the form-He wanted to have sex with his mother, therefore, added [the Oedipus complex, in this case] to his theory. As a matter of fact, almost all the perpetrators of inane arguments like the former, select romantic (sexual) partners in reaction to their neurotic parental relationship.

Psychoanalysis is now a historical curiosity. An obscurant pseudoscience that used ad-hoc explanations to particulars. However, the study has to be reclaimed and the empty barrages unveiled. Starting with its epistemic defence.

Empty Barrels-Argument via Falsification

Falsification has been the keystone to philosophy of science. Before, the problem of demarcation – as to differentiate science from non-science – had no satisfactory answer. As evident by its loose parlance, even by Freud.

It allowed for definite boundaries as to what science meant. Soon after, psychoanalysis came under attack. The Achilles heel being its unfalsifiable nature. While psychoanalysis remains unfalsifiable and a non-science, the inferred falseness? Merely a non-sequitur. For that another assumption is warranted, that science is the only road to epistemic certainty.

As Popper writes –

> Note that I suggest falsifiability as a criterion of demarcation, but not of meaning
>
> The Logic of Scientific Discovery, Karl Popper

The direct consequence of such an assumption is a complete disregard of non-sciences, including logic. A trivial example is the unfalsifiability of the proposition – All men are mortal. Concerning psychoanalysis, other difficulties follow. Namely that falsifying psychoanalytical propositions is impossible, for there exists nothing to be falsified.

Falsifiability requires propositions in the inter-subjective sphere. Such that if a claim is made, it can be disproved through evidence accessed here. For science, the inter-subjective space is empirical reality. In psychoanalysis, only the analysand has direct access to the evidence. Then indirectly communicated to the analyst and other individuals. The lack of an inter-subjective space makes it incoherent for falsifiability regarding psychoanalysis.

The Non-Proxy: Language

In The Epistemic Certainty of Language, I show the assumed certainty of language to be the maximal certainty possible in the inter-subjective sphere. Psychoanalysis, as Breuer put it, is the talking cure. Questioning the epistemic certainty of psychoanalysis is essentially questioning that of language. Even empirical science has to be communicated within language.

For the matters outside language, one cannot say anything of.

Epistemic validity of non-conscious thoughts must be considered. The unconscious ones, parapraxes and dreams, to aware non-conscious ones, the superego and other inner monologues. A variation of the Wittgensteinian private language argument suffices. As per the former, a true private language is impossible. Here, the existence of non-conscious thoughts with a sense reveals another part of our consciousness.

The Psychoanalytic Method

1. Collect fragments of the non-conscious. Both the strictly unconscious and aware non-conscious ones.
2. Retrieve the associated non-conscious thought in a state of uncontemplation.
3. As Freud explains, throughout his work, the state of uncontemplation happens when the analysand disassociates with the Ego. Such that no filtering prevents associated thoughts from being communicated, however repulsive they may be.
4. Analyst interprets the meaning, presents it, and seeks a response from the analysand.
5. Upon the correct interpretation, phenomenological certainty happens.

Non-Linguistic Certainty

The aim is to study the analysand and help them realize self-truths. Analysts acquire knowledge from the advancement of this pursuit. Thus, how does one know truths about oneself? If the maximal certainty possible in the inter-subjective sphere is of language, the (only) certainty possible in the pure subjective sphere is phenomenological certainty.

How can one know of happiness? What prompts the "Aha" of a long lost memory? What signals the reclamation of a parapraxis, the sudden remembrance of your lost keys? How does one know that one exists, the I knows that it's an I?

One simply knows. That is phenomenological certainty. As it cannot be reasoned through language, the incompatibility of the inter-subjective and pure subjectivity between, this is my defence. And the only required, and possible, one too.

A successful psychoanalytic treatment consists of such moments. When theories prompt the certainty of truth. Truth of the phenomenological kind, of the subjective kind.

A New Form of Beyond-Analysis

Psychoanalysis still has its limitations. The Guattarian-Deleuzian critique, the tradition's fixation on a lack (of desire) that an affirmative spirit of action-a Nietzschean outlook. Another is a possible oversight of phenomenology. Promising empirical results of Somatic Therapy, combined with its addression of the phenomenological unconscious leaves for consideration.

Thus, Beyond-Analysis would consist of two modalities-Phenomenological and Linguistic. Uniting the phenomenological approach of Somatism and the linguistic method of Psychoanalysis; although constructing it from the ground up, rooted in rigorous epistemology-ontology (The Epistemic Certainty of Language, Ontology of Meaning).

Moreover, beyond-analysis has the advantage of comprehensivity. Assuming the behaviorist assumptions, a focus on the unconscious lets the "right" emotions-behaviors emerge. If they are, in fact, our true ontological nature. Similar to (The Ethical Imperative).

To End

Unquestionably, the most theory-heavy essay of the book. Yet, still to be grappled with schizoanalytic-societal paradigms that contribute to neurosis; however, that is another tangent.

A Positive Project to the Death of God can't be built in one book.

References

Beck, Judith S. *Cognitive Behavior Therapy, Second Edition: Basics and Beyond.* 2011.

Mate, Gabor. *The Myth of Normal: Trauma, Illness, and Healing in a Toxic Culture.* 2022.

Popper, Karl. *The Logic of Scientific Discovery.* 1959.

Wittgenstein, Ludwig. *Philosophical Investigations.* 1953.

Epilogue

To keep this as concise as possible, that is my aim.

While writing the book, I changed considerably, the effect of psychoanalytic-somatic therapy, and along with it, the philosophy too. At first, the work was intended as a broad cultural critique, evident from the first section. However, once On Gender was completed, burnout had set in. Frustration, a result of an intentional focus on cultural critique aided by pop culture anecdotes, an approach validated by preliminary feedback I had received. I didn't desire this in the slightest. It felt like an implicit coercion into that style of writing, founded on motives of appeasement.

Transition, the movement to pure philosophy. Gradually, I started addressing problems in morality, language, and meaning, the ones that drew me into writing the book. Thus, setting the stage for the culmination, a beginning, in New Grounds. Still much theory to be flushed out, to be created.

As I'm writing the Epilogue, after the completion of a publisher review, certain clarifications are to be made. I have no interest in rewriting the essays, for their purpose was achieved, even in their mistakes, documentation of overcoming itself.

Fallacy of Experts

"More accurately, philosophy (and other social sciences) have no abstract methodological authority to fall back on."

In all fairness, even the "hard" sciences face the same problem. Replication crisis in the applied biological-chemical fields, neuroscience, psychology and the like. A stagnation of physics in finding any evidence for a unified theory. Inadequacy of Popper's falsification in discerning science from non-science. Perhaps the "problems" themselves require further explication.

I think that the task of philosophy is not to provide answers, but to show how the way we perceive a problem can be itself part of a problem

-Slavoj Zizek

"For that investigation one must await the advent of a new order of philosophers, such as will have other tastes and inclinations, the reverse of those hitherto prevalent–philosophers of the dangerous "Perhaps" in every sense of the term. And to speak in all seriousness, I see such new philosophers beginning to appear.

-Beyond Good and Evil (Nietzsche, 1886)

Thus, I have arrived."

While the arrogant grandiosity is appreciated, one must acknowledge other postmodernists, Foucault and Deleuze as examples.

On the Abuse of Happiness for Life

The Philosophical Argument Against the Active Paradigm, the argument of opposites and the descriptor lemma, functions through a characterization of happiness, specifically its pursuit, as culturally practiced. There are no innate claims, rather a critique. Although the point is emphasized later in the section, increased clarity does not harm.

"Such a contention arises due to the implicit nature of the happiness hypothesis. The simultaneous maximization and minimization of opposites, of happiness and suffering respectively."

The Metaphysics of Intoxicant

Like the Happiness Hypothesis, Metaphysics as culture conceives it to be; a quasi-satirical wording.

Ontology of Meaning

"Übermensch: The abstract beyond-individual (relative to the real current one) who transcends one or more essential fluxes, in contrast to the present one. An ever-moving imperishable anchor that enables becoming, one that perpetually exists, as long as one is alive. A Beautiful being with limitless potential, invigorating one with excitement, affirming life itself"

I have provided disclaimers of incomplete theory and a skepticism regarding the existence of essential fluxes before the chapter. Adding on, I am ever-skeptical at the moment whether any essential flux exists, that the lack of any essentiality is our "essential" property itself. However, more work is to be done.

The final chapter outlines the different projects that are to be pursued. Constructive projects of pure, dangerous philosophy.

1. Linguistic Epistemology-The namesake, a study of truth via language.
2. Flux Ontology-Nature of the human as explicit materialization of biological evolution.
3. Beyond-Analysis-A clinical methodology for ontological liberation, of the flux.

These one-liners are short, dense, and insufficiently explicit. And that is intentional. I cannot affirm any of these at the moment, certainly not the latter ones. To start with the initial project, and to see where I arrive. If it is willed, to develop the latter ones.

But here and there isolated and passionate cries are raised. How could they not be isolated when they deny what 'everybody knows .. ..?' And passionate, since they deny that which, it is said, nobody can deny? Such protest does not take place in the name of aristocratic prejudices: it is not a question of saying what few think and knowing what it means to think. On the contrary, it is a question of someone-if only one-with the necessary modesty not managing to know what everybody knows, and modestly denying what everybody is supposed to recognise.

-Difference and Repetition, Gilles Deleuze